William Shakespeare

THE TAMING OF THE SHREW

Edited by
David Bevington

David Scott Kastan,
James Hammersmith,
and Robert Kean Turner,
Associate Editors

With a Foreword by
Joseph Papp

W9-AXZ-494

BANTAM BOOKS
TORONTO / NEW YORK / LONDON / SYDNEY / AUCKLAND

THE TAMING OF THE SHREW

*A Bantam Book / published by arrangement
with Scott, Foresman and Company*

*PRINTING HISTORY
Scott, Foresman edition published / January 1980
Bantam edition, with newly edited text and substantially revised,
edited, and amplified notes, introductions, and other
materials, published / February 1988
Valuable advice on staging matters has been
provided by Richard Hosley.
Collations checked by Eric Rasmussen.
Additional editorial assistance by Claire McEachern.*

Library of Congress Cataloging-in-Publication Data

Shakespeare, William, 1564–1616.
   The taming of the shrew / William Shakespeare; edited by David
Bevington; David Scott Kastan, James Hammersmith, and Robert Kean
Turner, associate editors; with a foreword by Joseph Papp.
      p. cm.—(A Bantam classic)
   "Bantam edition with newly edited text and substantially revised,
edited, and amplified notes, introductions, and other materials"—
—T.p. verso.
   Bibliography: p.
   ISBN 0-553-21306-7 (pbk.)
   I. Bevington, David M.   II. Title.
PR2832.A2B44   1988
822.3′3—dc19   87–23195
                                                              CIP

Published simultaneously in the United States and Canada

PRINTED IN THE UNITED STATES OF AMERICA

O   0 9 8 7 6 5 4 3 2 1

WILLIAM SHAKESPEARE was born in Stratford-upon-Avon in April 1564, and his birth is traditionally celebrated on April 23. The facts of his life, known from surviving documents, are sparse. He was one of eight children born to John Shakespeare, a merchant of some standing in his community. William probably went to the King's New School in Stratford, but he had no university education. In November 1582, at the age of eighteen, he married Anne Hathaway, eight years his senior, who was pregnant with their first child, Susanna. She was born on May 26, 1583. Twins, a boy, Hamnet (who would die at age eleven), and a girl, Judith, were born in 1585. By 1592 Shakespeare had gone to London, working as an actor and already known as a playwright. A rival dramatist, Robert Greene, referred to him as "an upstart crow, beautified with our feathers." Shakespeare became a principal shareholder and playwright of the successful acting troupe the Lord Chamberlain's men (later, under James I, called the King's men). In 1599 the Lord Chamberlain's men built and occupied the Globe Theatre in Southwark near the Thames River. Here many of Shakespeare's plays were performed by the most famous actors of his time, including Richard Burbage, Will Kempe, and Robert Armin. In addition to his 37 plays, Shakespeare had a hand in others, including *Sir Thomas More* and *The Two Noble Kinsmen*, and he wrote poems, including *Venus and Adonis* and *The Rape of Lucrece*. His 154 sonnets were published, probably without his authorization, in 1609. In 1611 or 1612 he gave up his lodgings in London and devoted more and more of his time to retirement in Stratford, though he continued writing such plays as *The Tempest* and *Henry VIII* until about 1613. He died on April 23, 1616, and was buried in Holy Trinity Church, Stratford. No collected edition of his plays was published during his lifetime, but in 1623 two members of his acting company, John Heminges and Henry Condell, published the great collection now called the First Folio.

Bantam Shakespeare
The Complete Works—29 Volumes
Edited by David Bevington
With forewords by Joseph Papp on the plays

The Poems: Venus and Adonis, The Rape of Lucrece, The
Phoenix and Turtle, A Lover's Complaint,
the Sonnets

Antony and Cleopatra	*The Merchant of Venice*
As You Like It	*A Midsummer Night's Dream*
The Comedy of Errors	*Much Ado about Nothing*
Hamlet	*Othello*
Henry IV, Part One	*Richard II*
Henry IV, Part Two	*Richard III*
Henry V	*Romeo and Juliet*
Julius Caesar	*The Taming of the Shrew*
King Lear	*The Tempest*
Macbeth	*Twelfth Night*

Together in one volume:

Henry VI, Parts One, Two, and Three
King John and Henry VIII
*Measure for Measure, All's Well that Ends Well, and
Troilus and Cressida*
Three Early Comedies: Love's Labor's Lost, The Two
Gentlemen of Verona, The Merry
Wives of Windsor
Three Classical Tragedies: Titus Andronicus, Timon
of Athens, Coriolanus
The Late Romances: Pericles, Cymbeline, The Winter's
Tale, The Tempest

Two collections:

Four Comedies: The Taming of the Shrew, A Midsummer
Night's Dream, The Merchant of Venice,
Twelfth Night
Four Tragedies: Hamlet, Othello, King Lear, Macbeth

Contents

THE TAMING OF
THE SHREW

Foreword

It's hard to imagine, but Shakespeare wrote all of his plays with a quill pen, a goose feather whose hard end had to be sharpened frequently. How many times did he scrape the dull end to a point with his knife, dip it into the inkwell, and bring up, dripping wet, those wonderful words and ideas that are known all over the world?

In the age of word processors, typewriters, and ballpoint pens, we have almost forgotten the meaning of the word "blot." Yet when I went to school, in the 1930s, my classmates and I knew all too well what an inkblot from the metal-tipped pens we used would do to a nice clean page of a test paper, and we groaned whenever a splotch fell across the sheet. Most of us finished the school day with ink-stained fingers; those who were less careful also went home with ink-stained shirts, which were almost impossible to get clean.

When I think about how long it took me to write the simplest composition with a metal-tipped pen and ink, I can only marvel at how many plays Shakespeare scratched out with his goose-feather quill pen, year after year. Imagine him walking down one of the narrow cobblestoned streets of London, or perhaps drinking a pint of beer in his local alehouse. Suddenly his mind catches fire with an idea, or a sentence, or a previously elusive phrase. He is burning with impatience to write it down—but because he doesn't have a ballpoint pen or even a pencil in his pocket, he has to keep the idea in his head until he can get to his quill and parchment.

He rushes back to his lodgings on Silver Street, ignoring the vendors hawking brooms, the coaches clattering by, the piteous wails of beggars and prisoners. Bounding up the stairs, he snatches his quill and starts to write furiously, not even bothering to light a candle against the dusk. "To be, or not to be," he scrawls, "that is the—." But the quill point has gone dull, the letters have fattened out illegibly, and in the middle of writing one of the most famous passages in the history of dramatic literature, Shakespeare has to stop to sharpen his pen.

Taking a deep breath, he lights a candle now that it's dark, sits down, and begins again. By the time the candle has burned out and the noisy apprentices of his French Huguenot landlord have quieted down, Shakespeare has finished Act 3 of *Hamlet* with scarcely a blot.

Early the next morning, he hurries through the fog of a London summer morning to the rooms of his colleague Richard Burbage, the actor for whom the role of Hamlet is being written. He finds Burbage asleep and snoring loudly, sprawled across his straw mattress. Not only had the actor performed in *Henry V* the previous afternoon, but he had then gone out carousing all night with some friends who had come to the performance.

Shakespeare shakes his friend awake, until, bleary-eyed, Burbage sits up in his bed. "Dammit, Will," he grumbles, "can't you let an honest man sleep?" But the playwright, his eyes shining and the words tumbling out of his mouth, says, "Shut up and listen—tell me what you think of *this*!"

He begins to read to the still half-asleep Burbage, pacing around the room as he speaks. ". . . Whether 'tis nobler in the mind to suffer the slings and arrows of outrageous fortune—"

Burbage interrupts, suddenly wide awake, "That's excellent, very good, 'the slings and arrows of outrageous fortune,' yes, I think it will work quite well. . . ." He takes the parchment from Shakespeare and murmurs the lines to himself, slowly at first but with growing excitement.

The sun is just coming up, and the words of one of Shakespeare's most famous soliloquies are being uttered for the first time by the first actor ever to bring Hamlet to life. It must have been an exhilarating moment.

Shakespeare wrote most of his plays to be performed live by the actor Richard Burbage and the rest of the Lord Chamberlain's men (later the King's men). Today, however, our first encounter with the plays is usually in the form of the printed word. And there is no question that reading Shakespeare for the first time isn't easy. His plays aren't comic books or magazines or the dime-store detective novels I read when I was young. A lot of his sentences are complex. Many of his words are no longer used in our everyday

speech. His profound thoughts are often condensed into poetry, which is not as straightforward as prose.

Yet when you hear the words spoken aloud, a lot of the
language may strike you as unexpectedly modern. For
Shakespeare's plays, like any dramatic work, weren't really
meant to be read; they were meant to be spoken, seen, and
performed. It's amazing how lines that are so troublesome
in print can flow so naturally and easily when spoken.

I think it was precisely this music that first fascinated
me. When I was growing up, Shakespeare was a stranger to
me. I had no particular interest in him, for I was from a
different cultural tradition. It never occurred to me that his
plays might be more than just something to "get through"
in school, like science or math or the physical education
requirement we had to fulfill. My passions then were
movies, radio, and vaudeville—certainly not Elizabethan
drama.

I was, however, fascinated by words and language. Because I grew up in a home where Yiddish was spoken, and
English was only a second language, I was acutely sensitive
to the musical sounds of different languages and had an ear
for lilt and cadence and rhythm in the spoken word. And so
I loved reciting poems and speeches even as a very young
child. In first grade I learned lots of short nature verses—
"Who has seen the wind?," one of them began. My first
foray into drama was playing the role of Scrooge in Charles
Dickens's A Christmas Carol when I was eight years old. I
liked summoning all the scorn and coldness I possessed
and putting them into the words, "Bah, humbug!"

From there I moved on to longer and more famous poems
and other works by writers of the 1930s. Then, in junior
high school, I made my first acquaintance with Shakespeare through his play Julius Caesar. Our teacher, Miss
McKay, assigned the class a passage to memorize from the
opening scene of the play, the one that begins "Wherefore
rejoice? What conquest brings he home?" The passage
seemed so wonderfully theatrical and alive to me, and the
experience of memorizing and reciting it was so much fun,
that I went on to memorize another speech from the play on
my own.

I chose Mark Antony's address to the crowd in Act 3,

scene 2, which struck me then as incredibly high drama.
Even today, when I speak the words, I feel the same thrill I
did that first time. There is the strong and athletic Antony
descending from the raised pulpit where he has been speaking, right into the midst of a crowded Roman square. Hold-
ing the torn and bloody cloak of the murdered Julius
Caesar in his hand, he begins to speak to the people of
Rome:

> If you have tears, prepare to shed them now.
> You all do know this mantle. I remember
> The first time ever Caesar put it on;
> 'Twas on a summer's evening in his tent,
> That day he overcame the Nervii.
> Look, in this place ran Cassius' dagger through.
> See what a rent the envious Casca made.
> Through this the well-belovèd Brutus stabbed,
> And as he plucked his cursèd steel away,
> Mark how the blood of Caesar followed it,
> As rushing out of doors to be resolved
> If Brutus so unkindly knocked or no;
> For Brutus, as you know, was Caesar's angel.
> Judge, O you gods, how dearly Caesar loved him!
> This was the most unkindest cut of all . . .

I'm not sure now that I even knew Shakespeare had written a lot of other plays, or that he was considered "time-
less," "universal," or "classic"—but I knew a good speech
when I heard one, and I found the splendid rhythms of
Antony's rhetoric as exciting as anything I'd ever come
across.

Fifty years later, I still feel that way. Hearing good actors
speak Shakespeare gracefully and naturally is a wonderful
experience, unlike any other I know. There's a satisfying
fullness to the spoken word that the printed page just can't
convey. This is why seeing the plays of Shakespeare performed live in a theater is the best way to appreciate them.
If you can't do that, listening to sound recordings or watching film versions of the plays is the next best thing.

But if you do start with the printed word, use the play as a
script. Be an actor yourself and say the lines out loud. Don't
worry too much at first about words you don't immediately
understand. Look them up in the footnotes or a dictionary,

but don't spend too much time on this. It is more profitable (and fun) to get the sense of a passage and sing it out. Speak naturally, almost as if you were talking to a friend, but be sure to enunciate the words properly. You'll be surprised at how much you understand simply by speaking the speech "trippingly on the tongue," as Hamlet advises the Players.

You might start, as I once did, with a speech from *Julius Caesar*, in which the tribune (city official) Marullus scolds the commoners for transferring their loyalties so quickly from the defeated and murdered general Pompey to the newly victorious Julius Caesar:

> Wherefore rejoice? What conquest brings he home?
> What tributaries follow him to Rome
> To grace in captive bonds his chariot wheels?
> You blocks, you stones, you worse than senseless
>   things!
> O you hard hearts, you cruel men of Rome,
> Knew you not Pompey? Many a time and oft
> Have you climbed up to walls and battlements,
> To towers and windows, yea, to chimney tops,
> Your infants in your arms, and there have sat
> The livelong day, with patient expectation,
> To see great Pompey pass the streets of Rome.

With the exception of one or two words like "wherefore" (which means "why," not "where"), "tributaries" (which means "captives"), and "patient expectation" (which means patient waiting), the meaning and emotions of this speech can be easily understood.

From here you can go on to dialogues or other more challenging scenes. Although you may stumble over unaccustomed phrases or unfamiliar words at first, and even fall flat when you're crossing some particularly rocky passages, pick yourself up and stay with it. Remember that it takes time to feel at home with anything new. Soon you'll come to recognize Shakespeare's unique sense of humor and way of saying things as easily as you recognize a friend's laughter.

And then it will just be a matter of choosing which one of Shakespeare's plays you want to tackle next. As a true fan of his, you'll find that you're constantly learning from his plays. It's a journey of discovery that you can continue for the rest of your life. For no matter how many times you read or see a particular play, there will always be something new there that you won't have noticed before.

Why do so many thousands of people get hooked on Shakespeare and develop a habit that lasts a lifetime? What can he really say to us today, in a world filled with inventions and problems he never could have imagined? And how do you get past his special language and difficult sentence structure to understand him?

The best way to answer these questions is to go see a live production. You might not know much about Shakespeare, or much about the theater, but when you watch actors performing one of his plays on the stage, it will soon become clear to you why people get so excited about a playwright who lived hundreds of years ago.

For the story—what's happening in the play—is the most accessible part of Shakespeare. In *A Midsummer Night's Dream*, for example, you can immediately understand the situation: a girl is chasing a guy who's chasing a girl who's chasing another guy. No wonder *A Midsummer Night's Dream* is one of the most popular of Shakespeare's plays: it's about one of the world's most popular pastimes—falling in love.

But the course of true love never did run smooth, as the young suitor Lysander says. Often in Shakespeare's comedies the girl whom the guy loves doesn't love him back, or she loves him but he loves someone else. In *The Two Gentlemen of Verona*, Julia loves Proteus, Proteus loves Sylvia, and Sylvia loves Valentine, who is Proteus's best friend. In the end, of course, true love prevails, but not without lots of complications along the way.

For in all of his plays—comedies, histories, and tragedies—Shakespeare is showing you human nature. His characters act and react in the most extraordinary ways—and sometimes in the most incomprehensible ways. People are always trying to find motivations for what a character does. They ask, "Why does Iago want to destroy Othello?"

The answer, to me, is very simple—because that's the way Iago is. That's just his nature. Shakespeare doesn't explain his characters; he sets them in motion—and away they go. He doesn't worry about whether they're likable or not. He's interested in interesting people, and his most fascinating characters are those who are unpredictable. If you lean back in your chair early on in one of his plays, thinking you've figured out what Iago or Shylock (in *The Merchant of Venice*) is up to, don't be too sure—because that great judge of human nature, Shakespeare, will surprise you every time.

He is just as wily in the way he structures a play. In *Macbeth*, a comic scene is suddenly introduced just after the bloodiest and most treacherous slaughter imaginable, of a guest and king by his host and subject, when in comes a drunk porter who has to go to the bathroom. Shakespeare is tickling your emotions by bringing a stand-up comic on-stage right on the heels of a savage murder.

It has taken me thirty years to understand even some of these things, and so I'm not suggesting that Shakespeare is immediately understandable. I've gotten to know him not through theory but through practice, the practice of the *living* Shakespeare—the playwright of the theater.

Of course the plays are a great achievement of dramatic literature, and they should be studied and analyzed in schools and universities. But you must always remember, when reading all the words *about* the playwright and his plays, that *Shakespeare's* words came first and that in the end there is nothing greater than a single actor on the stage speaking the lines of Shakespeare.

Everything important that I know about Shakespeare comes from the practical business of producing and directing his plays in the theater. The task of classifying, criticizing, and editing Shakespeare's printed works I happily leave to others. For me, his plays really do live on the stage, not on the page. That is what he wrote them for and that is how they are best appreciated.

Although Shakespeare lived and wrote hundreds of years ago, his name rolls off my tongue as if he were my brother. As a producer and director, I feel that there is a professional relationship between us that spans the centuries. As a human being, I feel that Shakespeare has enriched my understanding of life immeasurably. I hope you'll let him do the same for you.

❖

Does *The Taming of the Shrew* have anything to say to us today, or is it hopelessly outdated by its male chauvinism? After all, here's a guy, Petruchio, who starves his wife, Kate, half to death, mocks and embarrasses her publicly, calls her "my goods, my chattels . . . my house, My household stuff, my field, my barn, My horse, my ox, my ass, my anything," and hurls verbal abuse at her—all in the name of taming her, the shrew. After a play full of this kind of treatment from her husband, Kate does indeed seem chastened: in her last speech she advises the other "froward wives" to honor and obey their men and acknowledges her own submission by putting her hand beneath Petruchio's foot. "Such duty as the subject owes the prince," she says, "Even such a woman oweth to her husband."

This is certainly bound to raise the hackles of many women, and even some men, who feel that Kate has betrayed the principles of the women's movement. But if we approach the play unburdened by present-day politics, we will find that the last speech is the culmination of a hard-fought and hard-won love between Kate and Petruchio, and that the notion of one-upmanship isn't part of the picture.

Shakespeare says quite plainly that if two people are really in love, the issue of who does what for whom does not exist. It's taken for granted in *The Taming of the Shrew* that Kate's last speech is certainly not the basis for their relationship, but will serve to bring out the best in Petruchio. Remember—Kate isn't the only one who has learned a lesson. The teacher Petruchio has also been a student and beneficiary of the painful lessons both have undergone.

On the stage, the playing is the thing. For example, when Meryl Streep and Raul Julia played Kate and Petruchio at the Delacorte Theater in Central Park, it was quite clear that the two characters cared for each other intensely. These wonderful actors entered the spirit of the play so wholeheartedly that they brought the characters to life and made what happens in the play totally believable.

Kate is one of Shakespeare's intelligent women who will not be pushed around. She is dumbfounded when Petruchio attempts to do just that. But his intention, as she discovers, is not to dominate but to rid her of an intractable manner she herself dislikes; he alone has the chutzpah to tackle her.

Petruchio deserves a medal for understanding Kate so well; instead, Shakespeare gave him a play!

JOSEPH PAPP GRATEFULLY ACKNOWLEDGES THE HELP OF

JOSEPH PAPP

JOSEPH PAPP GRATEFULLY ACKNOWLEDGES THE HELP OF ELIZABETH KIRKLAND IN PREPARING THIS FOREWORD.

Introduction

Like his other early comedies, *The Taming of the Shrew*
(c. 1592–1594) looks forward to Shakespeare's mature
comic drama in several ways. By skillfully juxtaposing two
plots and an induction, or framing plot, it offers contrasting
views on the nature of the love relationship will continue through many later
comedies. The play also adroitly manipulates the device of
mistaken identity, as in *The Comedy of Errors*, inverting
appearance and reality, dream and waking, and the master-
servant relationship in order to create a transformed Satur-
nalian world anticipating that of *A Midsummer Night's
Dream* and *Twelfth Night*.

The Induction sets up the theme of illusion, using an old
motif known as "The Sleeper Awakened" (as found for example in *The Arabian Nights*). This device frames the main
action of the play, giving to it an added perspective. *The
Taming of the Shrew* purports in fact to be a play within a
play, an entertainment devised by a witty nobleman as a
practical joke on a drunken tinker, Christopher Sly. The
jest is to convince Sly that he is not Sly at all, but an aristo-
crat suffering delusions. Outlandishly dressed in new finery, Sly is invited to witness a play from the gallery over the
stage. In a rendition called *The Taming of a Shrew* (printed
in 1594 and now generally thought to be taken from an earlier version of Shakespeare's play, employing a good deal of
conscious originality along with some literary borrowing
and even plagiarism), the framing plot concludes by actually putting Sly back out on the street in front of the alehouse where he was found. He awakes, recalls the play as a
dream, and proposes to put the vision to good use by taming
his own wife. Whether this ending reflects an epilogue now
lost from the text of Shakespeare's play cannot be said, but
it does reinforce the idea of the play as Sly's fantasy. Like
Puck at the end of *A Midsummer Night's Dream*, urging us
to dismiss what we have seen as the product of our own
slumbering, Sly continually reminds us that the play is only
an illusion or shadow.

With repeated daring, Shakespeare calls attention to the

contrived nature of his artifact, the play. When, for example, Sly is finally convinced that he is in fact a noble lord recovering from madness and lustily proposes to hasten off to bed with his long-neglected wife, we are comically aware that the "wife" is an impostor, a young page in disguise. Yet this counterfeiting of roles is no more unreal than the employment of Elizabethan boy-actors for the parts of Katharina and Bianca in the "real" play. As we watch Sly watching a play, levels of meaning interplay in this evocative fashion. Again, the paintings offered to Sly by his new attendants call attention to art's ability to confound illusion and reality. In one painting, Cytherea is hidden by reeds "Which seem to move and wanton with her breath / Even as the waving sedges play wi' th' wind," and in another painting Io appears "As lively painted as the deed was done" (Induction. 2.50–56). Sly's function, then, is that of the naive observer who inverts illusion and reality in his mind, concluding that his whole previous life of tinkers and alehouses and Cicely Hackets has been unreal. As his attendants explain to him, "These fifteen years you have been in a dream, / Or when you waked, so waked as if you slept" (79–80). We as audience laugh at Sly's naiveté, and yet we too are moved and even transformed by an artistic vision that we know to be illusory.

Like Sly, many characters in the main action of the play are persuaded, or nearly persuaded, to be what they are not. Lucentio and Tranio exchange roles of master and servant. Bianca's supposed tutors are in fact her wooers, using their lessons to disguise messages of love. Katharina is prevailed upon by her husband, Petruchio, to declare that the sun is the moon and that an old gentleman (Vincentio) is a fair young maiden. Vincentio is publicly informed that he is an impostor, and that the "real" Vincentio (the Pedant) is at that very moment looking at him out of the window of his son Lucentio's house. This last ruse does not fool the real Vincentio, but it nearly succeeds in fooling everyone else. Baptista Minola is about to commit Vincentio to jail for the infamous slander of asserting that the supposed Lucentio is only a servant in disguise. Vincentio, as the newly arrived stranger, is able to see matters as they really are; but the dwellers of Padua have grown so accustomed to the mad and improbable fictions of their life that they are not easily awakened to reality.

Shakespeare multiplies these devices of illusion by combining two entirely distinct plots, each concerned at least in part with the comic inversion of appearance and reality: the shrew-taming plot involving Petruchio and Kate, and the more conventional romantic plot involving Lucentio and Bianca. The latter plot is derived from the *Supposes* of George Gascoigne, a play first presented at Gray's Inn in 1566 as translated from Ariosto's neoclassical comedy *I Suppositi*, 1509. (Ariosto's work in turn was based upon Terence's *Eunuchus* and Plautus' *Captivi*.) The "Supposes" are mistaken identities or misunderstandings, the kind of hilarious farcical mix-ups Shakespeare had already experimented with in *The Comedy of Errors*. Shakespeare has, as usual, both romanticized his source and moralized it in a characteristically English way. The heroine, who in the Roman comedy of Plautus and Terence would have been a courtesan, and who in *Supposes* is made pregnant by her clandestine lover, remains thoroughly chaste in Shakespeare's comedy. Consequently she has no need for a pander, or go-between, such as the bawdy duenna, or nurse, of *Supposes*. The satire directed at the heroine's unwelcome old wooer is far less savage than in *Supposes*, where the "pantaloon," Dr. Cleander, is a villainously corrupt lawyer epitomizing the depravity of "respectable" society. Despite Shakespeare's modifications, however, the basic plot remains an effort to foil parental authority. The young lovers, choosing each other for romantic reasons, must fend off the materialistic calculations of their parents.

In a stock situation of this sort, the character types are also conventional. Gremio, the aged wealthy wooer, is actually labeled a "pantaloon" in the text (3.1.36–37) to stress his neoclassical ancestry. (Lean and foolish old wooers of this sort were customarily dressed in pantaloons, slippers, and spectacles on the Italian stage.) Gremio is typically "the graybeard," and Baptista Minola is "the narrow-prying father" (3.2.145–146). Even though Shakespeare renders these characters far less unattractive than in *Supposes*, their worldly behavior still invites reprisal from the young. Since Baptista Minola insists on selling his daughter Bianca to the highest bidder, it is fitting that her wealthiest suitor (the supposed Lucentio) should turn out in the end to be a penniless servant (Tranio) disguised as a man of affluence and position. In his traditional role as the clever servant of neoclassical comedy, Tranio skillfully apes the mannerisms of respectable society. He can deal in the mere surfaces, clothes or reputation, out of which a man's social importance is created, and can even furnish himself with a rich father. Gremio and Baptista deserve to be foiled because they accept the illusion of respectability as real.

Even the romantic lovers of this borrowed plot are largely conventional. To be sure, Shakespeare emphasizes their virtuous qualities and their sincerity. He adds Hortensio (not in *Supposes*) to provide Lucentio with a genuine, if foolish, rival and Bianca with two wooers closer to her age than old Gremio. Lucentio and Bianca deserve their romantic triumph; they are self-possessed, witty, and steadfast to each other. Yet we know very little about them, nor have they seen deeply into each other. Lucentio's love talk is laden with conventional images in praise of Bianca's dark eyes and scarlet lips. At the play's end, he discovers, to his surprise, that she can be willful, even disobedient. Has her appearance of virtue concealed something from him and from us? Because the relationship between these lovers is superficial, they are appropriately destined to a superficial marriage as well. The passive Bianca becomes the proud and defiant wife.

By contrast, Petruchio and Kate are the more interesting lovers, whose courtship involves mutual self-discovery. Admittedly, we must not overstate the case. Especially at first, these lovers are also stock types: the shrew tamer and his proverbially shrewish wife. Although Shakespeare seems not to have used any single source for this plot, he was well acquainted with crude misogynistic stories demonstrating the need for putting women in their place. In a ballad called *A Merry Jest of a Shrewd and Curst Wife Lapped in Morel's Skin* (printed c. 1550), for example, the husband tames his shrewish spouse by flaying her bloody with birch rods and then wrapping her in the freshly salted skin of a plow horse named Morel. (This shrewish wife, like Kate, has an obedient and gentle younger sister who is their father's favorite.)

Other features of Shakespeare's plot can be found in similar tales: the tailor scolded for devising a gown of outlandish fashion (Gerard Legh's *Accidence of Armory*, 1562), the wife obliged to agree with her husband's assertion of some patent falsehood (Don Juan Manuel's *El Conde Lucanor*, 1335), and the three husbands' wager on their wives' obedience (*The Book of the Knight of La Tour-Landry*, printed 1484). In the raw spirit of this sexist tradition, so unlike the refined Italianate sentiment of his other plot, Shakespeare introduces Petruchio as a man of reckless bravado who is ready to marry the ugliest or sharpest-tongued woman alive so long as she is rich. However much he may be later attracted by Kate's fiery spirit, his first attraction to her is crassly financial. Kate is, moreover, a thoroughly disagreeable young woman at first, described by those who know her as "intolerable curst / And shrewd, and froward" (1.2.88–89) and aggressive in her bullying of Bianca. She and Petruchio meet as grotesque comic counterparts. At the play's end, the traditional pattern of male dominance and female acquiescence is still prominent. Kate achieves peace only by yielding to a socially ordained patriarchal framework in which a husband is the princely ruler of his wife.

Within this male-oriented frame of reference, however, Petruchio and Kate are surprisingly like Benedick and Beatrice of *Much Ado about Nothing*. Petruchio, for all his rant, is increasingly drawn to Kate by her spirit. As wit-combatants they are worthy of each other's enmity—or love. No one else in the play is a fit match for either of them. Kate too is attracted to Petruchio, despite her war of words. Her guise of hostility is part defensive protection, part testing of his sincerity. If she is contemptuous of the wooers she has seen till now, she has good reason to be. We share her condescension toward the aged Gremio or the laughably inept Hortensio. She rightly fears that her father wishes to dispose of her so that he may auction off Bianca to the wealthiest competitor. Kate's jaded view of such marriage brokering is entirely defensible. Not surprisingly she first views Petruchio, whose professed intentions are far from reassuring, as another mere adventurer in love. She is impressed by his "line" in wooing her, but needs to test his constancy and sincerity. Possibly she is prepared to accept the prevailing Elizabethan view of marriage, with its dominant role for the husband, but only if she can choose a man deserving of her respect. She puts down most men with a shrewish manner that challenges their very masculinity; Petruchio is the first to be man enough to "board" her. Kate's rejection of men does not leave her very happy, however genuine her disdain is for most of those who come to woo. Petruchio's "schooling" is therefore curative. Having wooed and partly won her, he tests her with his late arrival at the marriage, his unconventional dress, and his crossing all her desires. In this display of willfulness, he shows her an ugly picture of what she herself is like. Most of all, however, he succeeds because he insists on what she too desires: a well-defined relationship tempered by mutual respect and love. Kate is visibly a more contented person at the play's end. Her closing speech, with its fine blend of irony and self-conscious hyperbole, together with its seriousness of concern, expresses beautifully the way in which Kate's independence of spirit and her newfound acceptance of a domestic role are successfully fused.

The Taming of the Shrew
in Performance

It is an odd kind of tribute to *The Taming of the Shrew* that it has inspired over the centuries so many adaptations and offshoots. Although Shakespeare's original play was popular in its own day and was kept in repertory seemingly through much of Shakespeare's lifetime, only in greatly altered forms did it enjoy stage success through much of the seventeenth, eighteenth, and early nineteenth centuries. These transformations were probably a response to the play's uncanny ability to make audiences of any era uncomfortable with its presentation of the war of the sexes.

Most adaptations seem to have had a twofold objective: to reinterpret the problematic taming and submission of Kate, and to do something with the unfinished Induction, or frame, of Christopher Sly. From the first, adapters of the play have felt a need to exaggerate, on both sides, the aggression between male and female. The anonymous *The Taming of a Shrew* (derived, sometime before 1594, from a now-lost early version of Shakespeare's play) specifies at one point that Ferando, the renamed Petruchio, is to enter *"with a piece of meat upon his dagger's point"*—presumably to terrorize Kate. Conversely, *The Woman's Prize, or The Tamer Tamed*, written by John Fletcher (Shakespeare's successor as chief dramatist to the acting company, the King's men) in 1611, provides a comic counterpart to the male victory in Shakespeare's play. In Fletcher's version Petruchio, remarried after Kate's death, meets his match in a woman who has nothing but scorn for tameness in wives. Petruchio has to learn to pacify his wife with gifts and is locked up and deceived by her, until a happy ending of sorts is worked out. Fletcher's premise, it would seem, is that the story of a husband's triumph in marriage ought to be answered by one in which the wife triumphs in her turn.

In subsequent adaptations, Shakespeare's portrayal of sexual warfare is pushed both toward further brutalizing the misogynistic elements (already present in Shakespeare's source, the ballad called *A Shrewd and Curst Wife*

Lapped in Morel's Skin) and toward giving the woman a chance to get back at her male tormentor. In *Sauny the Scot* by John Lacy, produced at the Drury Lane Theatre in 1667, Petruchio is indeed a brute. He threatens to whip Kate if she refuses him in marriage, insists she is suffering from a toothache so that he can summon a surgeon to pull one of her teeth, proclaims her dead and actually lashes her to her bier, and then complacently commends his wife when at last she submits to him. She is allowed only two lines to explain her views on the subject of obedience. The title of this adaptation comes from the name of Petruchio's comic servant (Grumio in Shakespeare), who speaks in such a broad Scottish dialect that Samuel Pepys, in 1667, had trouble understanding what was said. James Worsdale's *A Cure for a Scold* (Theatre Royal, Drury Lane, 1735, with Charles Macklin as Petruchio) retained much of Lacy's misogynistic humor, including the tooth-drawing episode. Lacy and Worsdale both provide their shrews with hints of reprisal: the women vow to tame their husbands if given a chance, and Worsdale's Peg Worthy (the renamed Kate, played by Kitty Clive) submits to her husband only after she has feigned death and thereby tricked him into demonstrating his affection for her. These versions by Lacy and Worsdale were immensely popular throughout the Restoration and the first half of the eighteenth century, eclipsing Shakespeare's original in the repertory.

Their popular successor, David Garrick's *Catharine and Petruchio,* held the stage without serious rival for nearly a century after its first performance in 1754 at Drury Lane. Like its predecessors, it at once brutalizes and intensifies the encounters of Kate and Petruchio. In order to focus on the warring lovers, Garrick eliminated both the Induction and the whole Bianca-Lucentio plot, and Kate's father, in this version, is unrelenting in his insistence that she marry or be disowned. It may have been Garrick who first gave Petruchio a whip; in any event, for decades afterward it was an obligatory prop. Yet Kate's speech after her wooing, in Act 1, includes a promise (or threat) of independence of spirit: "Sister Bianca now shall see / The poor abandoned Catharine, as she calls me, / Can hold her head as high, and be as proud, / And make her husband stoop unto her lure, / As she or e'er a wife in Padua." Garrick's instincts were sound in appraising the tastes of his day, for his shortened version (often part of a double bill) remained successful in England and America throughout the nineteenth century. In 1867, Henry Irving performed it with Ellen Terry at the Queen's Theatre, and in 1897 Herbert Beerbohm Tree presented Garrick's shortened version as an afterpiece for the opening night of Her Majesty's Theatre.

English audiences did not see a version close to Shakespeare's until 1844, when the play was produced by Benjamin Webster at the Haymarket Theatre with the Induction intact and with an attempt at Elizabethan costuming as conceived by J. R. Planché. The mise-en-scène was laid in a nobleman's hall as though for the entertainment of Christopher Sly, with no more scenery than could be supplied by two screens and a pair of curtains. Players in the Induction were made up to resemble playwrights Shakespeare and Ben Jonson and the actor Richard Tarlton. The dialogue of the play as a whole kept reasonably close to the original. In 1856 Samuel Phelps produced a slightly cut version of Shakespeare's text at the Sadler's Wells Theatre. He preserved the Induction (playing Sly himself), excised most of the play's bawdy, and softened Kate's character. The United States was provided with its first view of Shakespeare's play in 1887 by Augustin Daly at his theater in New York. The production featured handsome sets inspired by the painter Veronese and a commanding performance of Kate by Ada Rehan. In 1913 at the Prince of Wales Theatre, John Martin-Harvey, advised by William Poel, presented a robust, good-natured *Taming of the Shrew* that attempted to recreate the staging conventions of the Elizabethan theater.

Ever since being reestablished in its own right, *The Taming of the Shrew* has challenged actors and audiences alike to come to terms with its delicate balancing of misogyny and forbearance in marriage. Inevitably the critical point in a performance is the moment of Kate's final speech. How are we to take her gesture of submission? As early as 1908 in Melbourne, Australia, and then in 1914 in New York, Margaret Anglin delivered Kate's long speech on obedience with a mocking suggestion of a private understanding between her and her husband. Conversely, more conventional productions have succeeded with audiences that were still willing to enjoy a comedy of male triumph in the battle of the sexes. Oscillating between these poles of interpretation, the play has become something of a problem play. At the Shakespeare Festival performance in Ashland, Oregon, in 1977, when Petruchio refused to accept Kate's gesture of placing her hand beneath his foot and instead returned her cap to her, audiences were divided as to whether the belated gesture made up for all that Kate had undergone or was simply an attempt on the part of the acting company to be up-to-date.

The Royal Shakespeare Company, at Stratford-upon-Avon in 1978, confronted the potential offensiveness of Kate's submission by refusing to underplay the difficulty: Kate and the other women smouldered in resentment, while the men basked in complacency. One reviewer congratulated the director, Michael Bogdanov, on the honesty with which he tackled this "barbaric and disgusting" play. In 1975, at the Open Space Theatre in London, Charles Marowitz's adaptation called *The Shrew* had already taken this line of interpretation to its logical but frightening conclusion by playing the schooling of Kate as an illustration of the techniques of brainwashing. The ordeal ended in madness and rape for Katharina, and her final speech of submission was delivered as though by rote.

More temperately responsive to Shakespeare's text was the encounter of Meryl Streep and Raul Julia in Wilford Leach's production at the Delacorte Theatre in New York in 1978; Julia unabashedly called upon his own Latin American heritage of machismo to motivate Petruchio's way with women, while Streep, herself a modern woman, approached the role of Kate with the kind of ironic distance made possible by a self-aware and historical perspective. An ironic point of view gave to both actors a chance to enjoy role-playing and yet to preserve an essential part of their own integrity. In a 1960 production by the Royal Shakespeare Company, John Barton's direction of Peter O'Toole and Peggy Ashcroft, as Petruchio and Kate, stressed a good-natured playfulness between a man and a woman who obviously love each other from the start. Elizabeth Taylor and Richard Burton, in a very uneven film version by Franco Zeffirelli (1967), found in their best moments a modern idiom through which to explore the emotional nuances of an aggressive courtship; Taylor played Kate as a hot-tempered tomboy, understandably wary of male claims of prerogative, who has to decide how to respond to an attractive and virile man who seems to want her as a woman but whose motives are otherwise far from clear.

An entirely different strategy sometimes employed in modern productions is to downplay the complexities of the husband-wife issue and to focus instead on hilarity, as in the boisterous production at the Broadway Theatre in New York in 1935 starring Alfred Lunt and Lynn Fontaine, Clifford Williams's 1973 farce for the Royal Shakespeare Company, and a zany *commedia dell'arte* performance by the American Conservatory Theatre of San Francisco in 1976.

The Induction has required solutions as varied and ingenious as those for the wife-taming plot. The anonymous adaptation *The Taming of a Shrew* completed the framing plot of the Induction with an epilogue in which Sly awakens to find himself a beggar once again, ready to apply the lessons he has learned from the play to his own private life. In *Sauny the Scot* the Induction was simply left out. In 1716 Charles Johnson and Christopher Bullock went in the other direction in their nearly contemporaneous adaptations (both called *The Cobbler of Preston*) by making a whole short play out of the Induction. *A Cure for a Scold* and Garrick's *Catharine and Petruchio* also did without, so that the Induction was not often seen in conjunction with the rest of the play before Webster's revival of 1844. But even thereafter, Frank Benson omitted it in 1901 at the Comedy Theatre, as did William Bridges-Adams at Stratford-upon-Avon in 1919 and Dennis Carey, after opening night, at the Old Vic in 1954. Sir Barry Jackson, on the other hand, kept Sly and the Lord in view until the very end of the play, in one of the boxes, dressed in modern dress (Court Theatre, 1928). Ben Iden Payne at Stratford-upon-Avon in 1935 and Tyrone Guthrie at the Old Vic in 1939 similarly kept Sly onstage throughout.

The epilogue from *A Shrew* has been revived at times, as at the Old Vic in 1931 and at Stratford-upon-Avon in 1953. The Stratford Festival in Canada in the 1960s ended the play by having its performers, a band of strolling players, pack up and go off in search of another audience. The so-called Young Vic Company, on tour in the 1970s, conceived of Sly as a frustrated actor who eventually turns up in the play proper in the role of the Pedant, thus recalling a doubling effect used earlier at the New Theatre in 1937. Cole Porter's musical of 1948, *Kiss Me Kate*, converted the idea of a framing plot and a play-within-the-play into a story of actors whose tempestuous love life offstage reflects the difficulties of the wooers they portray.

Shakespeare's text calls for the second scene of the Induction to be played "aloft," that is, in the gallery at the back of the main stage, though the scene is longer, more elaborate, and more peopled with actors than is normal for action "above" in Shakespearean drama, and there is no interaction with persons below on the main stage as in most such scenes. If Sly were to continue to sit in the gallery throughout the play, his presence would complicate the staging of Act 5, scene 1, in which the gallery seems to be needed for a window in the house of Lucentio. In the anonymous *A Shrew*, where Sly does remain throughout, he appears to be situated at one side of the stage, not aloft. Shakespeare may have had to deal with varying theatrical conditions if the play was acted first in one theatre and then in another. We are not likely ever to know for certain how the Induction was staged in its original performances. In its own way, Shakespeare's Induction has remained as much a challenge to directors and actors of *The Taming of the Shrew* as has the battle for mastery between Petruchio and Kate.

The Playhouse

tectum

planities siue arena

proscænium

This early copy of a drawing by Johannes de Witt of the Swan Theatre in London (c. 1596), made by his friend Arend van Buchell, is the only surviving contemporary sketch of the interior of a public theater in the 1590s.

From other contemporary evidence, including the stage directions and dialogue of Elizabethan plays, we can surmise that the various public theaters where Shakespeare's plays were produced (the Theatre, the Curtain, the Globe) resembled the Swan in many important particulars, though there must have been some variations as well. The public playhouses were essentially round, or polygonal, and open to the sky, forming an acting arena approximately 70 feet in diameter; they did not have a large curtain with which to open and close a scene, such as we see today in opera and some traditional theater. A platform measuring approximately 43 feet across and 27 feet deep, referred to in the de Witt drawing as the *proscaenium*, projected into the yard, *planities sive arena*. The roof, *tectum*, above the stage and supported by two pillars, could contain machinery for ascents and descents, as were required in several of Shakespeare's late plays. Above this roof was a hut, shown in the drawing with a flag flying atop it and a trumpeter at its door announcing the performance of a play. The underside of the stage roof, called the heavens, was usually richly decorated with symbolic figures of the sun, the moon, and the constellations. The platform stage stood at a height of 5½ feet or so above the yard, providing room under the stage for underworldly effects. A trapdoor, which is not visible in this drawing, gave access to the space below.

The structure at the back of the platform (labeled *mimorum aedes*), known as the tiring-house because it was the actors' attiring (dressing) space, featured at least two doors, as shown here. Some theaters seem to have also had a discovery space, or curtained recessed alcove, perhaps between the two doors—in which Falstaff could have hidden from the sheriff (*1 Henry IV*, 2.4) or Polonius could have eavesdropped on Hamlet and his mother (*Hamlet*, 3.4). This discovery space probably gave the actors a means of access to and from the tiring-house. Curtains may also have been hung in front of the stage doors on occasion. The de Witt drawing shows a gallery above the doors that extends across the back and evidently contains spectators. On occasions when action "above" demanded the use of this space, as when Juliet appears at her "window" (*Romeo and Juliet*, 2.2 and 3.5), the gallery seems to have been used by the actors, but large scenes there were impractical.

The three-tiered auditorium is perhaps best described by Thomas Platter, a visitor to London in 1599 who saw on that occasion Shakespeare's *Julius Caesar* performed at the Globe:

> The playhouses are so constructed that they play on a raised platform, so that everyone has a good view. There are different galleries and places [*orchestra, sedilia, porticus*], however, where the seating is better and more comfortable and therefore more expensive. For whoever cares to stand below only pays one English penny, but if he wishes to sit, he enters by another door [*ingressus*] and pays another penny, while if he desires to sit in the most comfortable seats, which are cushioned, where he not only sees everything well but can also be seen, then he pays yet another English penny at another door. And during the performance food and drink are carried round the audience, so that for what one cares to pay one may also have refreshment.

Scenery was not used, though the theater building itself was handsome enough to invoke a feeling of order and hierarchy that lent itself to the splendor and pageantry onstage. Portable properties, such as thrones, stools, tables, and beds, could be carried or thrust on as needed. In the scene pictured here by de Witt, a lady on a bench, attended perhaps by her waiting-gentlewoman, receives the address of a male figure. If Shakespeare had written *Twelfth Night* by 1596 for performance at the Swan, we could imagine Malvolio appearing like this as he bows before the Countess Olivia and her gentlewoman, Maria.

THE TAMING OF
THE SHREW

Induction 1

*Enter beggar (Christopher Sly)
and Hostess.*

SLY   I'll feeze you, in faith.   1

HOSTESS   A pair of stocks, you rogue!   2

SLY   You're a baggage. The Slys are no rogues. Look in   3
the chronicles; we came in with Richard Conqueror.   4
Therefore *paucas pallabris*, let the world slide. Sessa!   5

HOSTESS   You will not pay for the glasses you have
burst?

SLY   No, not a denier. Go by, Saint Jeronimy, go to thy   8
cold bed and warm thee.   9

HOSTESS   I know my remedy; I must go fetch the third-   10
borough.   *[Exit.]*   11

SLY   Third, or fourth, or fifth borough, I'll answer him   12
by law. I'll not budge an inch, boy. Let him come, and
kindly.   *Falls asleep.*   14

*Wind horns [within]. Enter a Lord from hunting,
with his train.*

LORD
Huntsman, I charge thee, tender well my hounds.   15
Breathe Merriman—the poor cur is embossed—   16
And couple Clowder with the deep-mouthed brach.   17
Sawst thou not, boy, how Silver made it good
At the hedge corner, in the coldest fault?   19
I would not lose the dog for twenty pound.

FIRST HUNTSMAN
Why, Bellman is as good as he, my lord.

**Induction 1. Location: Before an alehouse, and subsequently before the
Lord's house nearby. (See ll. 75, 135.)**
1 feeze you i.e., fix you, get even with you   **2 A . . . stocks** i.e., I'll have
you put in the stocks   **3 baggage** contemptible woman or prostitute
4 Richard (Sly's mistake for "William.")   **5 paucas pallabris** i.e., *pocas
palabras*, "few words." (Spanish.)   **Sessa** (Of doubtful meaning; perhaps
"be quiet," "cease," or "let it go.")   **8 denier** French copper coin of
little value.   **Go . . . Jeronimy** (Sly's variation of an often-quoted line
from Kyd's *The Spanish Tragedy*, expressing impatience.)   **8–9 go . . .
thee** (Perhaps a proverb; see *King Lear* 3.4.46–47.)   **10–11 thirdborough**
constable   **12 Third** (Sly shows his ignorance; the *third* in "thirdborough" derives from the Old English word *frith*, "peace.")   **14 kindly**
welcome   **s.d. Wind** blow   **15 tender** care for   **16 embossed** foaming at
the mouth from exhaustion   **17 brach** bitch hound   **19 fault** loss of scent

He cried upon it at the merest loss,   22
And twice today picked out the dullest scent.
Trust me, I take him for the better dog.

LORD

Thou art a fool. If Echo were as fleet,
I would esteem him worth a dozen such.
But sup them well and look unto them all.
Tomorrow I intend to hunt again.

FIRST HUNTSMAN   I will, my lord.

LORD [*Seeing Sly*]

What's here? One dead, or drunk? See, doth he breathe?

SECOND HUNTSMAN [*Examining Sly*]

He breathes, my lord. Were he not warmed with ale,
This were a bed but cold to sleep so soundly.

LORD

O monstrous beast, how like a swine he lies!
Grim death, how foul and loathsome is thine image!   34
Sirs, I will practice on this drunken man.   35
What think you, if he were conveyed to bed,
Wrapped in sweet clothes, rings put upon his fingers, 37
A most delicious banquet by his bed,   38
And brave attendants near him when he wakes,   39
Would not the beggar then forget himself?

FIRST HUNTSMAN

Believe me, lord, I think he cannot choose.

SECOND HUNTSMAN

It would seem strange unto him when he waked.

LORD

Even as a flattering dream or worthless fancy.   43
Then take him up, and manage well the jest.
Carry him gently to my fairest chamber,
And hang it round with all my wanton pictures.
Balm his foul head in warm distillèd waters,
And burn sweet wood to make the lodging sweet.
Procure me music ready when he wakes
To make a dulcet and a heavenly sound.
And if he chance to speak, be ready straight,   51

22 **cried . . . loss** bayed to signal recovery of the scent after it had been
completely lost   34 **image** likeness (since sleep was regarded as a
likeness of death)   35 **practice on** play a joke on   37 **sweet** perfumed
38 **banquet** light repast   39 **brave** finely arrayed   43 **fancy** flight of
imagination   51 **straight** at once

And with a low submissive reverence
Say, "What is it your honor will command?"
Let one attend him with a silver basin
Full of rosewater and bestrewed with flowers;
Another bear the ewer, the third a diaper,   56
And say, "Will 't please your lordship cool your hands?"
Someone be ready with a costly suit
And ask him what apparel he will wear;
Another tell him of his hounds and horse,
And that his lady mourns at his disease.
Persuade him that he hath been lunatic,
And when he says he is, say that he dreams,
For he is nothing but a mighty lord.
This do, and do it kindly, gentle sirs.   65
It will be pastime passing excellent,   66
If it be husbanded with modesty.   67

FIRST HUNTSMAN
My lord, I warrant you we will play our part
As he shall think by our true diligence   69
He is no less than what we say he is.

LORD
Take him up gently and to bed with him,
And each one to his office when he wakes.   72
          [*Some bear out Sly.*] *Sound trumpets* [*within*].
Sirrah, go see what trumpet 'tis that sounds.   73
                    [*Exit Servingman.*]
Belike some noble gentleman that means,   74
Traveling some journey, to repose him here.

          Enter Servingman.

How now? Who is it?
SERVINGMAN   An 't please your honor, players
That offer service to your lordship.

          Enter Players.

LORD
Bid them come near.—Now, fellows, you are welcome.

---

56 ewer jug, pitcher.   **diaper** towel   **65 kindly** naturally (and thus
persuasively)   **66 passing** surpassingly   **67 husbanded with modesty**
managed with decorum   **69 As** so that   **72 office** duty   **73 Sirrah**
(Usual form of address to inferiors.)   **74 Belike** perhaps

PLAYERS   We thank your honor.

LORD
Do you intend to stay with me tonight?

FIRST PLAYER
So please your lordship to accept our duty.   81

LORD
With all my heart. This fellow I remember
Since once he played a farmer's eldest son.—
'Twas where you wooed the gentlewoman so well.
I have forgot your name, but sure that part
Was aptly fitted and naturally performed.

SECOND PLAYER
I think 'twas Soto that your honor means.

LORD
'Tis very true. Thou didst it excellent.
Well, you are come to me in happy time,   89
The rather for I have some sport in hand   90
Wherein your cunning can assist me much.
There is a lord will hear you play tonight.
But I am doubtful of your modesties,   93
Lest, overeyeing of his odd behavior—   94
For yet his honor never heard a play—
You break into some merry passion   96
And so offend him; for I tell you, sirs,
If you should smile he grows impatient.

FIRST PLAYER
Fear not, my lord, we can contain ourselves
Were he the veriest antic in the world.   100

LORD [*To a Servingman*]
Go, sirrah, take them to the buttery,   101
And give them friendly welcome every one.
Let them want nothing that my house affords.   103
                    Exit one with the Players.
Sirrah, go you to Barthol'mew my page,   104
And see him dressed in all suits like a lady.   105

---

81 duty expression of respect   **89 happy** opportune   **90 The rather for**
the more so since   **93 doubtful** apprehensive.   **modesties** discretion,
self-control   **94 overeyeing of** witnessing   **96 merry passion** outburst of
laughter   **100 antic** buffoon or eccentric   **101 buttery** pantry, or a room
for storing liquor (in butts) and other provisions   **103 want** lack
104 Barthol'mew (Pronounced "Bartlemy.")   **105 in all suits** in every
detail

That done, conduct him to the drunkard's chamber,
And call him "madam," do him obeisance.
Tell him from me, as he will win my love,   108
He bear himself with honorable action,
Such as he hath observed in noble ladies
Unto their lords, by them accomplishèd.
Such duty to the drunkard let him do
With soft low tongue and lowly courtesy,
And say, "What is 't your honor will command,
Wherein your lady and your humble wife
May show her duty and make known her love?"
And then with kind embracements, tempting kisses,
And with declining head into his bosom,
Bid him shed tears, as being overjoyed
To see her noble lord restored to health,
Who for this seven years hath esteemèd him   121
No better than a poor and loathsome beggar.
And if the boy have not a woman's gift
To rain a shower of commanded tears,
An onion will do well for such a shift,   125
Which in a napkin being close conveyed   126
Shall in despite enforce a watery eye.
See this dispatched with all the haste thou canst.
Anon I'll give thee more instructions.   129
                              Exit a Servingman.
I know the boy will well usurp the grace,   130
Voice, gait, and action of a gentlewoman.
I long to hear him call the drunkard husband,
And how my men will stay themselves from laughter
When they do homage to this simple peasant.
I'll in to counsel them. Haply my presence
May well abate the overmerry spleen   136
Which otherwise would grow into extremes.
                                        [*Exeunt.*]

                              ❧

108 him i.e., the page Bartholomew   **121 him** himself   **125 shift** purpose   **126 napkin** handkerchief.   **close** secretly   **129 Anon** soon   **130 usurp** assume   **136 spleen** mood. (The spleen was the supposed seat of laughter and anger.)

Induction 2

Enter aloft the drunkard [Sly], with Attendants; some with apparel, basin, and ewer and other appurtenances; and Lord.

SLY For God's sake, a pot of small ale. 1

FIRST SERVANT
   Will 't please your lordship drink a cup of sack? 2

SECOND SERVANT
   Will 't please your honor taste of these conserves? 3

THIRD SERVANT
   What raiment will your honor wear today?

SLY I am Christophero Sly, call not me "honor" nor "lordship." I ne'er drank sack in my life; and if you give me any conserves, give me conserves of beef. 7 Ne'er ask me what raiment I'll wear, for I have no more doublets than backs, no more stockings than 9 legs, nor no more shoes than feet—nay, sometimes more feet than shoes, or such shoes as my toes look through the overleather.

LORD
   Heaven cease this idle humor in your honor! 13
   O, that a mighty man of such descent,
   Of such possessions and so high esteem,
   Should be infusèd with so foul a spirit!

SLY What, would you make me mad? Am not I Christopher Sly, old Sly's son of Burton-heath, by birth a 18 peddler, by education a cardmaker, by transmutation 19 a bearherd, and now by present profession a tinker? 20 Ask Marian Hacket, the fat alewife of Wincot, if she 21

Induction 2. Location: A bedchamber in the Lord's house.
s.d. aloft i.e., in the gallery over the rear facade of the stage **1 small** weak (and therefore cheap) **2 sack** sweet Spanish wine (suited for a gentleman to drink) **3 conserves** candied fruit **7 conserves of beef** preserved (salted) beef **9 doublets** men's jackets **13 idle** vain, foolish. **humor** whim, fancy **18 Burton-heath** (Perhaps Barton-on-the-Heath, about sixteen miles from Stratford, the home of Shakespeare's aunt.) **19 cardmaker** maker of cards or combs used to prepare wool for spinning **20 bearherd** keeper of a performing bear. **tinker** pot-mender **21 Wincot** small village about four miles from Stratford. (The parish register shows that there were Hackets living there in 1591.)

know me not. If she say I am not fourteen pence on 22
the score for sheer ale, score me up for the lyingest 23
knave in Christendom. What, I am not bestraught: 24
here's—

THIRD SERVANT
O, this it is that makes your lady mourn!

SECOND SERVANT
O, this is it that makes your servants droop!

LORD
Hence comes it that your kindred shuns your house,
As beaten hence by your strange lunacy.   29
O noble lord, bethink thee of thy birth,
Call home thy ancient thoughts from banishment,   31
And banish hence these abject lowly dreams.
Look how thy servants do attend on thee,
Each in his office ready at thy beck.
Wilt thou have music? Hark, Apollo plays,   *Music.* 35
And twenty cagèd nightingales do sing.
Or wilt thou sleep? We'll have thee to a couch,
Softer and sweeter than the lustful bed
On purpose trimmed up for Semiramis.   39
Say thou wilt walk; we will bestrew the ground.
Or wilt thou ride? Thy horses shall be trapped,   41
Their harness studded all with gold and pearl.
Dost thou love hawking? Thou hast hawks will soar
Above the morning lark. Or wilt thou hunt?
Thy hounds shall make the welkin answer them   45
And fetch shrill echoes from the hollow earth.

FIRST SERVANT
Say thou wilt course, thy greyhounds are as swift   47
As breathèd stags, ay, fleeter than the roe.   48

SECOND SERVANT
Dost thou love pictures? We will fetch thee straight
Adonis painted by a running brook,   50

22–23 on the score in debt (since such reckonings were originally
notched or scored on a stick)   **23 sheer** nothing but.   **score me up for**
reckon me to be   **24 bestraught** distracted   **29 As** as if   **31 ancient**
former   **35 Apollo** i.e., as god of music   **39 Semiramis** legendary queen
of Assyria famous for her voluptuousness   **41 trapped** adorned
45 welkin sky, heavens   **47 course** hunt the hare   **48 breathèd** in good
physical condition, with good wind.   **roe** small, swift deer   **50 Adonis** a
young huntsman with whom Venus is vainly in love. (See Shakespeare's
poem *Venus and Adonis*.)

And Cytherea all in sedges hid,   51
Which seem to move and wanton with her breath,   52
Even as the waving sedges play wi' th' wind.

LORD
We'll show thee Io as she was a maid,   54
And how she was beguilèd and surprised,
As lively painted as the deed was done.

THIRD SERVANT
Or Daphne roaming through a thorny wood,   57
Scratching her legs that one shall swear she bleeds,
And at that sight shall sad Apollo weep,
So workmanly the blood and tears are drawn.   60

LORD
Thou art a lord and nothing but a lord.
Thou hast a lady far more beautiful
Than any woman in this waning age.   63

FIRST SERVANT
And till the tears that she hath shed for thee
Like envious floods o'errun her lovely face,   65
She was the fairest creature in the world;
And yet she is inferior to none.   67

SLY
Am I a lord? And have I such a lady?
Or do I dream? Or have I dreamed till now?
I do not sleep: I see, I hear, I speak,
I smell sweet savors, and I feel soft things.
Upon my life, I am a lord indeed,
And not a tinker nor Christopher Sly.
Well, bring our lady hither to our sight,
And once again a pot o' the smallest ale.

SECOND SERVANT
Will 't please your mightiness to wash your hands?
O, how we joy to see your wit restored!   77
O, that once more you knew but what you are!

---

51 Cytherea one of the names for Venus (because of her association
with the island of Cythera). **sedges** grassy marsh plants   **52 wanton**
play seductively   **54 Io** one of Jupiter's lovers, transformed by him into
a heifer to conceal her from the envious Juno   **57 Daphne** a wood
nymph beloved by Apollo, changed by Diana into a laurel tree to preserve her from Apollo's assault   **60 workmanly** skillfully   **63 waning**
degenerate   **65 envious** spiteful   **67 yet** even today   **77 wit** mental
faculties, senses

These fifteen years you have been in a dream,
Or when you waked, so waked as if you slept.

SLY
  These fifteen years! By my fay, a goodly nap.   81
  But did I never speak of all that time?   82

FIRST SERVANT
  O, yes, my lord, but very idle words;
  For though you lay here in this goodly chamber,
  Yet would you say ye were beaten out of door,
  And rail upon the hostess of the house,   86
  And say you would present her at the leet,   87
  Because she brought stone jugs and no sealed quarts.   88
  Sometimes you would call out for Cicely Hacket.

SLY   Ay, the woman's maid of the house.

THIRD SERVANT
  Why, sir, you know no house nor no such maid,
  Nor no such men as you have reckoned up,
  As Stephen Sly, and old John Naps of Greece,   93
  And Peter Turf, and Henry Pimpernel,
  And twenty more such names and men as these,
  Which never were nor no man ever saw.

SLY
  Now Lord be thankèd for my good amends!   97

ALL
  Amen.

         Enter [*the Page as a*] *lady, with Attendants.*

SLY   I thank thee. Thou shalt not lose by it.

PAGE
  How fares my noble lord?

SLY   Marry, I fare well,   99
  For here is cheer enough. Where is my wife?

PAGE
  Here, noble lord. What is thy will with her?

---

81 fay faith   **82 of** during   **86 house** tavern   **87 present** bring accusa-
tion against.   **leet** manorial court   **88 sealed quarts** quart containers
officially stamped as a guarantee of that capacity   **93 Stephen . . .**
Greece (A Stephen Sly lived in Stratford during Shakespeare's day.
Greece is an apparent error for *Greet*, a Gloucestershire hamlet not far
from Stratford.)   **97 amends** recovery   **99 Marry** A mild oath, derived
from "by Mary."

SLY
  Are you my wife and will not call me husband?
  My men should call me "lord"; I am your goodman.   103
PAGE
  My husband and my lord, my lord and husband,
  I am your wife in all obedience.
SLY
  I know it well.—What must I call her?
LORD   Madam.
SLY Al'ce madam, or Joan madam?
LORD
  Madam, and nothing else. So lords call ladies.
SLY
  Madam wife, they say that I have dreamed
  And slept above some fifteen year or more.
PAGE
  Ay, and the time seems thirty unto me,
  Being all this time abandoned from your bed.   112
SLY
  'Tis much. Servants, leave me and her alone.
  Madam, undress you and come now to bed.
PAGE
  Thrice-noble lord, let me entreat of you
  To pardon me yet for a night or two,
  Or, if not so, until the sun be set.
  For your physicians have expressly charged,
  In peril to incur your former malady,
  That I should yet absent me from your bed.
  I hope this reason stands for my excuse.
SLY Ay, it stands so that I may hardly tarry so long. But 122
  I would be loath to fall into my dreams again. I will
  therefore tarry in despite of the flesh and the blood.

     Enter a [Servant as] messenger.

SERVANT
  Your honor's players, hearing your amendment,
  Are come to play a pleasant comedy;
  For so your doctors hold it very meet,   127
  Seeing too much sadness hath congealed your blood,

---

103 goodman (A homely term for "husband.") **112 abandoned** banished **122 stands** is the case (with bawdy pun) **127 meet** suitable

And melancholy is the nurse of frenzy.
Therefore they thought it good you hear a play
And frame your mind to mirth and merriment,
Which bars a thousand harms and lengthens life.

SLY   Marry, I will, let them play it. Is not a comonty a   133
Christmas gambold or a tumbling-trick?   134

PAGE
No, my good lord, it is more pleasing stuff.

SLY   What, household stuff?

PAGE   It is a kind of history.   137

SLY   Well, we'll see 't. Come, madam wife, sit by my
side and let the world slip; we shall ne'er be younger.

                    [*They sit over the stage.*] *Flourish.*

133, 134 comonty, gambold (Sly's words for *comedy* and *gambol.*)
137 history story

1.1   *Enter Lucentio and his man Tranio.*

LUCENTIO
   Tranio, since for the great desire I had
   To see fair Padua, nursery of arts,   2
   I am arrived for fruitful Lombardy,   3
   The pleasant garden of great Italy,
   And by my father's love and leave am armed
   With his good will and thy good company,
   My trusty servant, well approved in all,   7
   Here let us breathe and haply institute   8
   A course of learning and ingenious studies.   9
   Pisa, renownèd for grave citizens,
   Gave me my being, and my father first,   11
   A merchant of great traffic through the world,   12
   Vincentio, come of the Bentivolii.
   Vincentio's son, brought up in Florence,
   It shall become to serve all hopes conceived   15
   To deck his fortune with his virtuous deeds.   16
   And therefore, Tranio, for the time I study,
   Virtue and that part of philosophy
   Will I apply that treats of happiness   19
   By virtue specially to be achieved.
   Tell me thy mind, for I have Pisa left
   And am to Padua come, as he that leaves
   A shallow plash to plunge him in the deep   23
   And with satiety seeks to quench his thirst.
TRANIO
   Mi perdonate, gentle master mine,   25
   I am in all affected as yourself,   26
   Glad that you thus continue your resolve

1.1. Location: Padua. A street before Baptista's house.
2 Padua . . . arts (Padua's was one of the most renowned of universities during Shakespeare's time.)   **3 am arrived for** have arrived at. (Padua is not in Lombardy, but imprecise maps may have allowed Shakespeare to think of Lombardy as comprising all of northern Italy.)   **7 approved** tested and proved trustworthy   **8 breathe** pause, remain. **institute** begin   **9 ingenious** i.e., "ingenuous," liberal, befitting a well-born person   **11 first** i.e., before me   **12 of great traffic** involved in extensive trade   **15 It . . . conceived** i.e., it will befit me, Lucentio, to fulfill all the hopes entertained for me by my friends and relatives   **16 deck** adorn **19 apply** study.   **treats of** discusses, concerns   **23 plash** pool   **25 Mi perdonate** pardon me   **26 affected** disposed

To suck the sweets of sweet philosophy.
Only, good master, while we do admire
This virtue and this moral discipline,
Let's be no stoics nor no stocks, I pray,   31
Or so devote to Aristotle's checks   32
As Ovid be an outcast quite abjured.   33
Balk logic with acquaintance that you have,   34
And practice rhetoric in your common talk;
Music and poesy use to quicken you;   36
The mathematics and the metaphysics,
Fall to them as you find your stomach serves you.   38
No profit grows where is no pleasure ta'en.
In brief, sir, study what you most affect.   40

LUCENTIO
Gramercies, Tranio, well dost thou advise.   41
If, Biondello, thou wert come ashore,   42
We could at once put us in readiness,
And take a lodging fit to entertain
Such friends as time in Padua shall beget.
But stay awhile, what company is this?

TRANIO
Master, some show to welcome us to town.   47

*Enter Baptista with his two daughters Katharina
and Bianca, Gremio a pantaloon, [and] Hortensio
suitor to Bianca. Lucentio [and] Tranio stand by.*

BAPTISTA
Gentlemen, importune me no farther,
For how I firmly am resolved you know:
That is, not to bestow my youngest daughter
Before I have a husband for the elder.
If either of you both love Katharina,

---

31 stocks wooden posts, devoid of feeling (with a play on *stoics*)
32 devote devoted. **checks** restraints **33 As** so that. **Ovid** Latin love
poet (used here to typify amorous light entertainment as contrasted
with the serious philosophic study of Aristotle) **34 Balk logic** argue,
bandy words **36 quicken** refresh **38 stomach** inclination, appetite
40 affect find pleasant **41 Gramercies** many thanks **42 Biondello**
(Lucentio apostrophizes his absent servant.) **come ashore** (Padua,
though inland, is given a harbor by Shakespeare, unless he is thinking
of the canals that crossed northern Italy in the sixteenth century.)
47 s.d. pantaloon foolish old man, a stock character in Italian comedy

Because I know you well and love you well,
Leave shall you have to court her at your pleasure.

GREMIO

To cart her rather; she's too rough for me.   55
There, there, Hortensio, will you any wife?

KATHARINA [*To Baptista*]

I pray you, sir, is it your will
To make a stale of me amongst these mates?   58

HORTENSIO

"Mates," maid? How mean you that? No mates for you,
Unless you were of gentler, milder mold.

KATHARINA

I' faith, sir, you shall never need to fear:
Iwis it is not halfway to her heart.   62
But if it were, doubt not her care should be
To comb your noddle with a three-legged stool,
And paint your face, and use you like a fool.   65

HORTENSIO

From all such devils, good Lord deliver us!

GREMIO   And me too, good Lord!

TRANIO [*Aside to Lucentio*]

Husht, master, here's some good pastime toward.   68
That wench is stark mad or wonderful froward.   69

LUCENTIO [*Aside to Tranio*]

But in the other's silence do I see
Maid's mild behavior and sobriety.
Peace, Tranio!

TRANIO [*Aside to Lucentio*]

Well said, master; mum, and gaze your fill.

BAPTISTA

Gentlemen, that I may soon make good
What I have said—Bianca, get you in,
And let it not displease thee, good Bianca,
For I will love thee ne'er the less, my girl.

---

55 cart carry in a cart through the streets by way of punishment or public exposure (with a play on *court*)   **58 stale** laughingstock (with a play on the meaning "harlot," since a harlot might well be carted). **mates** rude fellows. (But Hortensio takes the word in the sense of "husband.")   **62 Iwis** indeed.   **it** i.e., marriage.   **her** i.e., my, Kate's   **65 paint** i.e., make red with scratches   **68 toward** in prospect **69 froward** perverse

KATHARINA   A pretty peat! It is best   78
  Put finger in the eye, an she knew why.   79

BIANCA
  Sister, content you in my discontent.—
  Sir, to your pleasure humbly I subscribe.
  My books and instruments shall be my company,
  On them to look and practice by myself.

LUCENTIO [Aside to Tranio]
  Hark, Tranio, thou mayst hear Minerva speak.   84

HORTENSIO
  Signor Baptista, will you be so strange?   85
  Sorry am I that our good will effects
  Bianca's grief.

GREMIO   Why will you mew her up,   87
  Signor Baptista, for this fiend of hell,
  And make her bear the penance of her tongue?   89

BAPTISTA
  Gentlemen, content ye; I am resolved.
  Go in, Bianca.   [Exit Bianca.]
  And for I know she taketh most delight   92
  In music, instruments, and poetry,
  Schoolmasters will I keep within my house
  Fit to instruct her youth. If you, Hortensio,
  Or Signor Gremio, you, know any such,
  Prefer them hither; for to cunning men   97
  I will be very kind, and liberal
  To mine own children in good bringing up.
  And so farewell.—Katharina, you may stay,
  For I have more to commune with Bianca.   Exit. 101

KATHARINA
  Why, and I trust I may go too, may I not?
  What, shall I be appointed hours,
  As though, belike, I knew not what to take,
  And what to leave? Ha!   Exit.

GREMIO   You may go to the devil's dam. Your gifts are 106
  so good, here's none will hold you.—Their love is not 107

---

78 peat darling, pet   **79 Put . . . eye** i.e., weep.   **an** if   **84 Minerva**
goddess of wisdom   **85 strange** distant, estranged   **87 mew** coop (as
one would a falcon)   **89 her . . . her** i.e., Bianca . . . Katharina's   **92 for**
because   **97 Prefer** recommend.   **cunning** skillful, learned   **101 commune** discuss   **106 dam** mother   **107 Their love** i.e., men's love of
women

so great, Hortensio, but we may blow our nails to- 108
gether, and fast it fairly out. Our cake's dough on both 109
sides. Farewell. Yet, for the love I bear my sweet
Bianca, if I can by any means light on a fit man to
teach her that wherein she delights, I will wish him to 112
her father.

HORTENSIO So will I, Signor Gremio. But a word, I
pray. Though the nature of our quarrel yet never
brooked parle, know now, upon advice, it toucheth us 116
both—that we may yet again have access to our fair
mistress and be happy rivals in Bianca's love—to labor
and effect one thing specially.

GREMIO What's that, I pray?

HORTENSIO Marry, sir, to get a husband for her sister.

GREMIO A husband? A devil.

HORTENSIO I say a husband.

GREMIO I say a devil. Think'st thou, Hortensio, though
her father be very rich, any man is so very a fool to be 125
married to hell?

HORTENSIO Tush, Gremio, though it pass your patience
and mine to endure her loud alarums, why, man, 128
there be good fellows in the world, an a man could
light on them, would take her with all faults, and
money enough.

GREMIO I cannot tell; but I had as lief take her dowry 132
with this condition, to be whipped at the high cross 133
every morning.

HORTENSIO Faith, as you say, there's small choice in
rotten apples. But come, since this bar in law makes 136
us friends, it shall be so far forth friendly maintained
till by helping Baptista's eldest daughter to a husband
we set his youngest free for a husband, and then have
to 't afresh. Sweet Bianca! Happy man be his dole! He 140

108–109 **blow . . . together** i.e., twiddle our thumbs, wait patiently
109 **fast . . . out** abstain as best we can.   **Our cake's dough** i.e., we're
out of luck, getting nowhere   112 **wish** commend   116 **brooked parle**
tolerated conference.   **advice** reflection.   **toucheth** concerns   125 **very**
utterly   128 **alarums** i.e., loud, startling noises. (A military metaphor.)
132 **had as lief** would as willingly   133 **high cross** cross set on a pedes-
tal in a marketplace or center of a town   136 **bar in law** obstruction to
our (legal) cause   140 **Happy . . . dole** i.e., may happiness be the reward
of him who wins. (Proverbial.)

that runs fastest gets the ring. How say you, Signor ¹⁴¹
Gremio?

GREMIO I am agreed, and would I had given him the
best horse in Padua to begin his wooing that would
thoroughly woo her, wed her, and bed her and rid the
house of her! Come on.   *Exeunt ambo.* ¹⁴⁶
                    Manent Tranio and Lucentio.

TRANIO
  I pray, sir, tell me, is it possible
  That love should of a sudden take such hold?

LUCENTIO
  O Tranio, till I found it to be true,
  I never thought it possible or likely.
  But see, while idly I stood looking on,
  I found the effect of love in idleness,   152
  And now in plainness do confess to thee,
  That art to me as secret and as dear   154
  As Anna to the Queen of Carthage was,   155
  Tranio, I burn, I pine, I perish, Tranio,
  If I achieve not this young modest girl.
  Counsel me, Tranio, for I know thou canst;
  Assist me, Tranio, for I know thou wilt.

TRANIO
  Master, it is no time to chide you now.
  Affection is not rated from the heart.   161
  If love have touched you, naught remains but so,
  "Redime te captum quam queas minimo."   163

LUCENTIO
  Gramercies, lad. Go forward. This contents;
  The rest will comfort, for thy counsel's sound.

TRANIO
  Master, you looked so longly on the maid,   166
  Perhaps you marked not what's the pith of all.   167

---

141 the ring (An allusion to the sport of riding at the ring, with quibble
on "wedding ring.") **146 s.d. ambo** both. **Manent** they remain onstage **152 love in idleness** the flower heartsease or pansy, to which was
attributed magical power in love. (See *A Midsummer Night's Dream*,
2.1.168.) **154 secret** trusted, intimate **155 Anna** confidante of her
sister Dido, Queen of Carthage, beloved of Aeneas **161 rated** driven
away by chiding **163 Redime . . . minimo** buy yourself out of bondage
for as little as you can. (From Terence's *Eunuchus* as quoted in Lily's
Latin Grammar.) **166 so longly** for such a long time; perhaps, also, so
longingly **167 pith** core, essence

LUCENTIO

  O, yes, I saw sweet beauty in her face,

  Such as the daughter of Agenor had,   169

  That made great Jove to humble him to her hand,   170

  When with his knees he kissed the Cretan strand.   171

TRANIO

  Saw you no more? Marked you not how her sister

  Began to scold and raise up such a storm

  That mortal ears might hardly endure the din?

LUCENTIO

  Tranio, I saw her coral lips to move,

  And with her breath she did perfume the air.

  Sacred and sweet was all I saw in her.

TRANIO [*Aside*]

  Nay, then, 'tis time to stir him from his trance.—

  I pray, awake, sir. If you love the maid,

  Bend thoughts and wits to achieve her. Thus it stands:

  Her elder sister is so curst and shrewd   181

  That till the father rid his hands of her,

  Master, your love must live a maid at home,

  And therefore has he closely mewed her up,

  Because she will not be annoyed with suitors.   185

LUCENTIO

  Ah, Tranio, what a cruel father's he!

  But art thou not advised he took some care   187

  To get her cunning schoolmasters to instruct her?

TRANIO

  Ay, marry, am I, sir; and now 'tis plotted.

LUCENTIO

  I have it, Tranio.

TRANIO   Master, for my hand,   190

  Both our inventions meet and jump in one.   191

LUCENTIO

  Tell me thine first.

TRANIO   You will be schoolmaster,

  And undertake the teaching of the maid:

  That's your device.

---

169 daughter of Agenor Europa, beloved of Jupiter, who took the form
of a bull in order to abduct her   **170 him** himself   **171 kissed** i.e., knelt
on   **181 curst** shrewish. **shrewd** ill-natured   **185 Because** so that
187 advised aware   **190 for my hand** for my part, i.e., it's my guess
191 inventions plans. **jump** tally, agree

LUCENTIO   It is. May it be done?

TRANIO
Not possible; for who shall bear your part,
And be in Padua here Vincentio's son,
Keep house and ply his book, welcome his friends,
Visit his countrymen, and banquet them?

LUCENTIO
Basta, content thee, for I have it full.   199
We have not yet been seen in any house,
Nor can we be distinguished by our faces
For man or master. Then it follows thus:
Thou shalt be master, Tranio, in my stead,
Keep house, and port, and servants, as I should.   204
I will some other be, some Florentine,
Some Neapolitan, or meaner man of Pisa.   206
'Tis hatched and shall be so. Tranio, at once
Uncase thee. Take my colored hat and cloak.   208
When Biondello comes, he waits on thee,
But I will charm him first to keep his tongue.   210

TRANIO   So had you need.
In brief, sir, sith it your pleasure is,   212
And I am tied to be obedient—
For so your father charged me at our parting,
"Be serviceable to my son," quoth he,
Although I think 'twas in another sense—
I am content to be Lucentio,
Because so well I love Lucentio.

> [*They exchange clothes.*]

LUCENTIO
Tranio, be so, because Lucentio loves.
And let me be a slave, t' achieve that maid
Whose sudden sight hath thralled my wounded eye.   221

> *Enter Biondello.*

Here comes the rogue.—Sirrah, where have you been?

BIONDELLO
Where have I been? Nay, how now, where are you?

---

199 Basta enough.   **full** i.e., fully thought out   **204 port** state, style of
living   **206 meaner** of a lower social class   **208 Uncase** i.e., remove hat
and cloak.   **colored** (as opposed to blue generally worn by servants; see
4.1.81)   **210 charm** i.e., persuade   **212 sith** since   **221 Whose sudden
sight** i.e., the sudden sight of whom

Master, has my fellow Tranio stol'n your clothes?
Or you stol'n his? Or both? Pray, what's the news?

LUCENTIO

Sirrah, come hither. 'Tis no time to jest,
And therefore frame your manners to the time.
Your fellow Tranio here, to save my life,
Puts my apparel and my countenance on,   229
And I for my escape have put on his;
For in a quarrel since I came ashore
I killed a man, and fear I was descried.   232
Wait you on him, I charge you, as becomes,   233
While I make way from hence to save my life.
You understand me?

BIONDELLO   I, sir?—Ne'er a whit.   235

LUCENTIO

And not a jot of Tranio in your mouth.
Tranio is changed into Lucentio.

BIONDELLO

The better for him. Would I were so too!

TRANIO

So could I, faith, boy, to have the next wish after,
That Lucentio indeed had Baptista's youngest daughter.
But, sirrah, not for my sake, but your master's, I advise
You use your manners discreetly in all kind of compa-
  nies.
When I am alone, why, then I am Tranio,
But in all places else your master Lucentio.

LUCENTIO   Tranio, let's go.
One thing more rests, that thyself execute: 246
To make one among these wooers. If thou ask me why,
Sufficeth my reasons are both good and weighty.   248

                                        Exeunt.

        The presenters above speak.

FIRST SERVANT

My lord, you nod. You do not mind the play.   249

---

229 countenance bearing, manner   **232 descried** observed   **233 as
becomes** as is suitable   **235 I, sir** (Lucentio may hear this as "Ay,
sir.")   **246 rests** remains to be done   **248 Sufficeth** it suffices that
s.d. presenters characters of the Induction, whose role it is to "present"
the play proper   **249 mind** attend to

SLY   Yes, by Saint Anne, do I. A good matter, surely.
Comes there any more of it?

PAGE [*As Lady*]   My lord, 'tis but begun.

SLY   'Tis a very excellent piece of work, madam lady;
would 'twere done!   *They sit and mark.* 254

1.2   *Enter Petruchio and his man Grumio.*

PETRUCHIO
    Verona, for a while I take my leave
    To see my friends in Padua, but of all
    My best belovèd and approvèd friend,
    Hortensio; and I trow this is his house.   4
    Here, sirrah Grumio, knock, I say.

GRUMIO   Knock, sir? Whom should I knock? Is there any
man has rebused your worship?   7

PETRUCHIO   Villain, I say, knock me here soundly.   8

GRUMIO   Knock you here, sir? Why, sir, what am I, sir,
that I should knock you here, sir?

PETRUCHIO
    Villain, I say, knock me at this gate,   11
    And rap me well, or I'll knock your knave's pate.

GRUMIO
    My master is grown quarrelsome. I should knock you
      first,
    And then I know after who comes by the worst.

PETRUCHIO   Will it not be?
    Faith, sirrah, an you'll not knock, I'll ring it.   16
    I'll try how you can *sol fa*, and sing it.   17
                   He wrings him by the ears.

GRUMIO
    Help, masters, help! My master is mad.

PETRUCHIO
    Now knock when I bid you, sirrah villain.

254 s.d. mark observe

1.2. Location: Padua. Before Hortensio's house.
4 trow believe   **7 rebused** (A blunder for *abused*.)   **8 me** i.e., for me.
(But Grumio, perhaps intentionally, misunderstands.)   **11 gate** door
16 ring sound loudly, using a circular knocker (with a pun on *wring*)
17 I'll . . . sing it i.e., I'll make you cry out, howl

Enter Hortensio.

HORTENSIO How now, what's the matter? My old friend
 Grumio, and my good friend Petruchio? How do you
 all at Verona?

PETRUCHIO
 Signor Hortensio, come you to part the fray?
 Con tutto il cuore, ben trovato, may I say.   24

HORTENSIO
 Alla nostra casa ben venuto,   25
 Molto onorato signor mio Petruchio.—   26
 Rise, Grumio, rise. We will compound this quarrel. 27

GRUMIO Nay, 'tis no matter, sir, what he 'leges in Latin. 28
 If this be not a lawful cause for me to leave his service!
 Look you, sir: he bid me knock him and rap him
 soundly, sir. Well, was it fit for a servant to use his
 master so, being perhaps, for aught I see, two-and- 32
 thirty, a pip out?   33
 Whom would to God I had well knocked at first,
 Then had not Grumio come by the worst.

PETRUCHIO
 A senseless villain! Good Hortensio,
 I bade the rascal knock upon your gate,
 And could not get him for my heart to do it.

GRUMIO Knock at the gate? O heavens! Spake you not
 these words plain, "Sirrah, knock me here, rap me
 here, knock me well, and knock me soundly"? And
 come you now with "knocking at the gate"?

PETRUCHIO
 Sirrah, begone, or talk not, I advise you.

HORTENSIO
 Petruchio, patience, I am Grumio's pledge.   44
 Why, this's a heavy chance twixt him and you, 45
 Your ancient, trusty, pleasant servant Grumio. 46
 And tell me now, sweet friend, what happy gale
 Blows you to Padua here from old Verona?

---

24 Con . . . trovato with all my heart, well met **25–26 Alla . . . Petruchio** welcome to our house, my much honored Petruchio. (Italian.)
27 compound settle **28 'leges** alleges **32–33 two . . . out** i.e., drunk.
(Derived from the card game called *one-and-thirty*.) **33 pip** a spot on a
playing card. (Hence *a pip out* means "off by one," or "one in excess of
thirty-one.") **44 pledge** surety **45 heavy chance** sad occurrence
46 ancient long-standing

PETRUCHIO
  Such wind as scatters young men through the world
  To seek their fortunes farther than at home,
  Where small experience grows. But in a few,   51
  Signor Hortensio, thus it stands with me:
  Antonio, my father, is deceased,
  And I have thrust myself into this maze,
  Haply to wive and thrive as best I may.
  Crowns in my purse I have, and goods at home,
  And so am come abroad to see the world.

HORTENSIO
  Petruchio, shall I then come roundly to thee   58
  And wish thee to a shrewd ill-favored wife?
  Thou'dst thank me but a little for my counsel.
  And yet I'll promise thee she shall be rich,
  And very rich. But thou'rt too much my friend,
  And I'll not wish thee to her.

PETRUCHIO
  Signor Hortensio, twixt such friends as we
  Few words suffice. And therefore, if thou know
  One rich enough to be Petruchio's wife—
  As wealth is burden of my wooing dance—   67
  Be she as foul as was Florentius' love,   68
  As old as Sibyl, and as curst and shrewd   69
  As Socrates' Xanthippe, or a worse,   70
  She moves me not, or not removes, at least,
  Affection's edge in me, were she as rough
  As are the swelling Adriatic seas.
  I come to wive it wealthily in Padua;
  If wealthily, then happily in Padua.

GRUMIO   Nay, look you, sir, he tells you flatly what his
  mind is. Why, give him gold enough and marry him   77

---

51 in a few in short   **58 come roundly** speak plainly   **67 burden** undersong, i.e., basis   **68 foul** ugly.   **Florentius' love** (An allusion to Gower's
version in *Confessio Amantis* of the fairy tale of the knight who promised to marry an ugly old woman if she solved the riddle he must
answer. After the fulfillment of all promises, she became young and
beautiful. Another version of this story is Chaucer's "Tale of the Wife of
Bath," from *The Canterbury Tales*.)   **69 Sibyl** prophetess of Cumae to
whom Apollo gave as many years of life as she held grains of sand in
her hand   **70 Xanthippe** the philosopher's notoriously shrewish wife
77 mind intention

to a puppet or an aglet-baby, or an old trot with ne'er 78
a tooth in her head, though she have as many diseases
as two-and-fifty horses. Why, nothing comes amiss, so
money comes withal.   81

HORTENSIO
  Petruchio, since we are stepped thus far in,
  I will continue that I broached in jest.   83
  I can, Petruchio, help thee to a wife
  With wealth enough, and young and beauteous,
  Brought up as best becomes a gentlewoman.
  Her only fault, and that is faults enough,
  Is that she is intolerable curst
  And shrewd, and froward, so beyond all measure
  That, were my state far worser than it is,   90
  I would not wed her for a mine of gold.

PETRUCHIO
  Hortensio, peace! Thou know'st not gold's effect.
  Tell me her father's name and 'tis enough;
  For I will board her though she chide as loud   94
  As thunder when the clouds in autumn crack.

HORTENSIO
  Her father is Baptista Minola,
  An affable and courteous gentleman.
  Her name is Katharina Minola,
  Renowned in Padua for her scolding tongue.

PETRUCHIO
  I know her father, though I know not her,
  And he knew my deceasèd father well.
  I will not sleep, Hortensio, till I see her;
  And therefore let me be thus bold with you
  To give you over at this first encounter,   104
  Unless you will accompany me thither.

GRUMIO [To Hortensio] I pray you, sir, let him go while
the humor lasts. O' my word, an she knew him as well 107
as I do, she would think scolding would do little good
upon him. She may perhaps call him half a score

---

78 aglet-baby small figure carved on the tag of a lace.   **trot** old hag;
also, prostitute **81 withal** with it **83 that** what **90 state** estate
94 board accost. (A metaphor from naval warfare.) **104 give you over**
leave you **107 humor** whim

knaves or so. Why, that's nothing; an he begin once, he'll rail in his rope tricks. I'll tell you what, sir, an 111 she stand him but a little, he will throw a figure in her 112 face and so disfigure her with it that she shall have no more eyes to see withal than a cat. You know him not, sir.

HORTENSIO
Tarry, Petruchio, I must go with thee,
For in Baptista's keep my treasure is.   117
He hath the jewel of my life in hold,   118
His youngest daughter, beautiful Bianca,
And her withholds from me and other more,   120
Suitors to her and rivals in my love,
Supposing it a thing impossible,
For those defects I have before rehearsed,
That ever Katharina will be wooed.
Therefore this order hath Baptista ta'en,
That none shall have access unto Bianca
Till Katharine the curst have got a husband.

GRUMIO   Katharine the curst!
A title for a maid of all titles the worst.

HORTENSIO
Now shall my friend Petruchio do me grace,   130
And offer me disguised in sober robes
To old Baptista as a schoolmaster
Well seen in music, to instruct Bianca,   133
That so I may by this device at least
Have leave and leisure to make love to her,   135
And unsuspected court her by herself.

*Enter Gremio [with a paper], and Lucentio
disguised [as a schoolmaster].*

GRUMIO   Here's no knavery! See, to beguile the old folks, how the young folks lay their heads together! Master, master, look about you. Who goes there, ha?

---

111 rope tricks i.e., a blunder for "rhetricks," i.e., rhetoric (?) or tricks worthy of hanging (?)   **112 stand** withstand.   **figure** figure of speech
117 keep keeping (with suggestion of "fortified place" where one would store a treasure)   **118 hold** confinement (with a similar pun on "stronghold")   **120 other** others   **130 grace** a favor   **133 seen** skilled
135 make love to woo

HORTENSIO
  Peace, Grumio, it is the rival of my love.
  Petruchio, stand by awhile.   [*They stand aside.*]
GRUMIO [*Aside*]
  A proper stripling and an amorous!   142
GREMIO [*To Lucentio*]
  O, very well, I have perused the note.   143
  Hark you, sir, I'll have them very fairly bound—
  All books of love, see that at any hand—   145
  And see you read no other lectures to her.   146
  You understand me. Over and besides
  Signor Baptista's liberality,
  I'll mend it with a largess. Take your paper too,   149
                  [*Giving Lucentio the note*]
  And let me have them very well perfumed,   150
  For she is sweeter than perfume itself
  To whom they go to. What will you read to her?
LUCENTIO
  Whate'er I read to her, I'll plead for you
  As for my patron, stand you so assured,
  As firmly as yourself were still in place—
  Yea, and perhaps with more successful words   155
  Than you, unless you were a scholar, sir.
GREMIO
  O this learning, what a thing it is!
GRUMIO [*Aside*]
  O this woodcock, what an ass it is!   159
PETRUCHIO   Peace, sirrah!
HORTENSIO [*Coming forward*]
  Grumio, mum!—God save you, Signor Gremio.
GREMIO
  And you are well met, Signor Hortensio.
  Trow you whither I am going? To Baptista Minola. 163
  I promised to inquire carefully
  About a schoolmaster for the fair Bianca,
  And by good fortune I have lighted well

---

142 proper stripling handsome young fellow. (Said ironically, in reference to Gremio.) **143 note** (Evidently, a list of books for Bianca's tutoring.) **145 at any hand** in any case **146 read . . . lectures** teach no other lessons **149 mend** improve, increase. **largess** gift of money **150 them** i.e., the books **155 as** as if. **in place** present **159 woodcock** (A bird easily caught; proverbially stupid.) **163 Trow** know

On this young man—for learning and behavior
Fit for her turn, well read in poetry
And other books, good ones, I warrant ye.

HORTENSIO
'Tis well. And I have met a gentleman
Hath promised me to help me to another,   171
A fine musician to instruct our mistress.
So shall I no whit be behind in duty
To fair Bianca, so beloved of me.

GREMIO
Beloved of me, and that my deeds shall prove.

GRUMIO [Aside]   And that his bags shall prove.   176

HORTENSIO
Gremio, 'tis now no time to vent our love.   177
Listen to me, and if you speak me fair,   178
I'll tell you news indifferent good for either.   179
Here is a gentleman whom by chance I met,
Upon agreement from us to his liking,   181
Will undertake to woo curst Katharine,
Yea, and to marry her, if her dowry please.

GREMIO   So said, so done, is well.
Hortensio, have you told him all her faults?

PETRUCHIO
I know she is an irksome brawling scold.
If that be all, masters, I hear no harm.

GREMIO
No, sayst me so, friend? What countryman?

PETRUCHIO
Born in Verona, old Antonio's son.
My father dead, my fortune lives for me,
And I do hope good days and long to see.

GREMIO
O sir, such a life with such a wife were strange.
But if you have a stomach, to 't i' God's name.
You shall have me assisting you in all.
But will you woo this wildcat?

PETRUCHIO   Will I live?

---

171 Hath who has   176 bags moneybags   177 vent express   178 fair
civilly, courteously   179 indifferent equally   181 Upon . . . liking who,
on terms agreeable to him. (In ll. 213–214 we learn that Bianca's suitors
will *bear his charge of wooing*.)

GRUMIO [*Aside*]
  Will he woo her? Ay, or I'll hang her.
PETRUCHIO
  Why came I hither but to that intent?
  Think you a little din can daunt mine ears?
  Have I not in my time heard lions roar?
  Have I not heard the sea, puffed up with winds,
  Rage like an angry boar chafèd with sweat?
  Have I not heard great ordnance in the field,   202
  And heaven's artillery thunder in the skies?
  Have I not in a pitchèd battle heard
  Loud 'larums, neighing steeds, and trumpets' clang?   205
  And do you tell me of a woman's tongue,
  That gives not half so great a blow to hear
  As will a chestnut in a farmer's fire?
  Tush, tush! Fear boys with bugs.
GRUMIO [*Aside*]   For he fears none.   209
GREMIO Hortensio, hark.
  This gentleman is happily arrived,   211
  My mind presumes, for his own good and ours.
HORTENSIO
  I promised we would be contributors
  And bear his charge of wooing whatsoe'er.   214
GREMIO
  And so we will, provided that he win her.
GRUMIO [*Aside*]
  I would I were as sure of a good dinner.   216

      Enter Tranio brave [*as Lucentio*], *and Biondello.*

TRANIO
  Gentlemen, God save you. If I may be bold,
  Tell me, I beseech you, which is the readiest way
  To the house of Signor Baptista Minola?
BIONDELLO He that has the two fair daughters, is 't he
  you mean?
TRANIO Even he, Biondello.
GREMIO
  Hark you, sir, you mean not her to—

---

202 ordnance artillery **205 'larums** calls to arms **209 Fear . . . bugs**
frighten children with bugbears, bogeymen **211 happily** fortunately,
just when needed **214 charge** expense **216 s.d. brave** elegantly
dressed

TRANIO
   Perhaps him and her, sir. What have you to do?   224

PETRUCHIO
   Not her that chides, sir, at any hand, I pray.

TRANIO
   I love no chiders, sir. Biondello, let's away.

LUCENTIO [*Aside*]
   Well begun, Tranio.

HORTENSIO   Sir, a word ere you go.
   Are you a suitor to the maid you talk of, yea or no?

TRANIO
   An if I be, sir, is it any offense?

GREMIO
   No, if without more words you will get you hence.

TRANIO
   Why, sir, I pray, are not the streets as free
   For me as for you?

GREMIO   But so is not she.

TRANIO
   For what reason, I beseech you?

GREMIO   For this reason, if you'll know,
   That she's the choice love of Signor Gremio.

HORTENSIO
   That she's the chosen of Signor Hortensio.

TRANIO
   Softly, my masters! If you be gentlemen,
   Do me this right: hear me with patience.
   Baptista is a noble gentleman,
   To whom my father is not all unknown;
   And were his daughter fairer than she is,
   She may more suitors have, and me for one.
   Fair Leda's daughter had a thousand wooers;   242
   Then well one more may fair Bianca have,
   And so she shall. Lucentio shall make one,
   Though Paris came in hope to speed alone.   245

GREMIO
   What, this gentleman will outtalk us all.

---

224 him and her i.e., both Baptista Minola and his daughter. **What . . . do** what's that to you **242 Leda's daughter** Helen of Troy **245 Though** even if. **Paris** Trojan prince who abducted Helen from her husband, Menelaus. **speed** succeed

LUCENTIO
  Sir, give him head. I know he'll prove a jade.   247
PETRUCHIO
  Hortensio, to what end are all these words?
HORTENSIO [*To Tranio*]
  Sir, let me be so bold as ask you,
  Did you yet ever see Baptista's daughter?
TRANIO
  No, sir, but hear I do that he hath two,
  The one as famous for a scolding tongue
  As is the other for beauteous modesty.
PETRUCHIO
  Sir, sir, the first's for me. Let her go by.
GREMIO
  Yea, leave that labor to great Hercules,
  And let it be more than Alcides' twelve.   256
PETRUCHIO
  Sir, understand you this of me, in sooth: 257
  The youngest daughter, whom you hearken for,   258
  Her father keeps from all access of suitors,
  And will not promise her to any man
  Until the elder sister first be wed.
  The younger then is free, and not before.
TRANIO
  If it be so, sir, that you are the man
  Must stead us all, and me amongst the rest;   264
  And if you break the ice and do this feat,
  Achieve the elder, set the younger free
  For our access, whose hap shall be to have her   267
  Will not so graceless be to be ingrate.
HORTENSIO
  Sir, you say well, and well you do conceive.   269
  And since you do profess to be a suitor,
  You must, as we do, gratify this gentleman,   271
  To whom we all rest generally beholding.   272

---

247 prove a jade tire like an ill-conditioned horse **256 Alcides'** descendant of Alcaeus (i.e., Hercules, who, noted for the achievement of the twelve great labors, is the only one capable of conquering Katharina) **257 sooth** truth **258 hearken for** lie in wait for, seek to win **264 Must stead** who must help **267 whose hap** he whose good fortune **269 conceive** understand **271 gratify** reward, requite **272 beholding** beholden, indebted

TRANIO
　　Sir, I shall not be slack, in sign whereof,
　　Please ye we may contrive this afternoon   274
　　And quaff carouses to our mistress' health,   275
　　And do as adversaries do in law,   276
　　Strive mightily, but eat and drink as friends.

GRUMIO, BIONDELLO
　　O excellent motion! Fellows, let's be gone.   278

HORTENSIO
　　The motion's good indeed, and be it so.
　　Petruchio, I shall be your *ben venuto*.   *Exeunt.*　280

❧

---

274 contrive spend, pass (time)　**275 quaff carouses** drink toasts
276 adversaries opposing lawyers　**278 motion** suggestion　**280 ben
venuto** welcome, i.e., host

2.1   *Enter Katharina and Bianca [with her hands tied].*

BIANCA
Good sister, wrong me not, nor wrong yourself,
To make a bondmaid and a slave of me.
That I disdain. But for these other goods,   3
Unbind my hands, I'll pull them off myself,
Yea, all my raiment, to my petticoat,
Or what you will command me will I do,
So well I know my duty to my elders.

KATHARINA
Of all thy suitors, here I charge thee, tell
Whom thou lov'st best. See thou dissemble not.

BIANCA
Believe me, sister, of all the men alive
I never yet beheld that special face
Which I could fancy more than any other.

KATHARINA
Minion, thou liest. Is 't not Hortensio?   13

BIANCA
If you affect him, sister, here I swear   14
I'll plead for you myself but you shall have him.

KATHARINA
O, then belike you fancy riches more:
You will have Gremio to keep you fair.   17

BIANCA
Is it for him you do envy me so?
Nay, then, you jest, and now I well perceive
You have but jested with me all this while.
I prithee, sister Kate, untie my hands.

KATHARINA
If that be jest, then all the rest was so.

                                        Strikes her.

     Enter Baptista.

BAPTISTA
Why, how now, dame, whence grows this insolence?—

2.1. Location: Padua. Baptista's house.
3 goods possessions   **13 Minion** hussy   **14 affect** love   **17 fair** resplendent with finery

Bianca, stand aside. Poor girl, she weeps.
Go ply thy needle, meddle not with her.—
For shame, thou hilding of a devilish spirit, 26
Why dost thou wrong her that did ne'er wrong thee?
When did she cross thee with a bitter word?

KATHARINA
Her silence flouts me, and I'll be revenged.
Flies after Bianca.

BAPTISTA
What, in my sight? Bianca, get thee in.
Exit [Bianca].

KATHARINA
What, will you not suffer me? Nay, now I see
She is your treasure, she must have a husband;
I must dance barefoot on her wedding day, 33
And for your love to her lead apes in hell. 34
Talk not to me. I will go sit and weep
Till I can find occasion of revenge. *[Exit.]*

BAPTISTA
Was ever gentleman thus grieved as I?
But who comes here? 38

*Enter Gremio, Lucentio [as a schoolmaster] in the
habit of a mean man, Petruchio, with [Hortensio
as a musician, and] Tranio [as Lucentio] with his
boy [Biondello] bearing a lute and books.*

GREMIO Good morrow, neighbor Baptista.
BAPTISTA Good morrow, neighbor Gremio. God save
you, gentlemen.
PETRUCHIO
And you, good sir. Pray, have you not a daughter
Called Katharina, fair and virtuous?
BAPTISTA
I have a daughter, sir, called Katharina.
GREMIO
You are too blunt. Go to it orderly.
PETRUCHIO
You wrong me, Signor Gremio; give me leave.—

---

26 hilding vicious (hence worthless) beast **33, 34 dance . . . day, lead
. . . hell** (Popularly supposed to be the fate of old maids.) **38 s.d. mean**
of low social station. (Said here of a schoolmaster.)

I am a gentleman of Verona, sir,
That, hearing of her beauty and her wit,
Her affability and bashful modesty,
Her wondrous qualities and mild behavior,
Am bold to show myself a forward guest
Within your house, to make mine eye the witness
Of that report which I so oft have heard.
And, for an entrance to my entertainment,   54
I do present you with a man of mine,

        [*Presenting Hortensio*]

Cunning in music and the mathematics,
To instruct her fully in those sciences,   57
Whereof I know she is not ignorant.
Accept of him, or else you do me wrong.
His name is Litio, born in Mantua.

BAPTISTA
You're welcome, sir, and he, for your good sake.
But for my daughter Katharine, this I know,
She is not for your turn, the more my grief.

PETRUCHIO
I see you do not mean to part with her,
Or else you like not of my company.

BAPTISTA
Mistake me not, I speak but as I find.
Whence are you, sir? What may I call your name?

PETRUCHIO
Petruchio is my name, Antonio's son,
A man well known throughout all Italy.

BAPTISTA
I know him well. You are welcome for his sake.   70

GREMIO
Saving your tale, Petruchio, I pray,   71
Let us that are poor petitioners speak too.
Bacare! You are marvelous forward.   73

PETRUCHIO
O, pardon me, Signor Gremio, I would fain be doing.   74

---

54 entrance entrance fee. **entertainment** reception **57 sciences** subjects, branches of knowledge **70 know** know of (see also l. 105)
71 Saving with all due respect for **73 Bacare** stand back **74 fain** gladly. **doing** getting on with the business (with sexual suggestion)

GREMIO

I doubt it not, sir, but you will curse your wooing.—
Neighbors, this is a gift very grateful, I am sure of it. [*To*
Baptista.] To express the like kindness, myself, that have
been more kindly beholding to you than any, freely give
unto you this young scholar [*Presenting Lucentio*],
that hath been long studying at Rheims, as cunning
in Greek, Latin, and other languages as the other in
music and mathematics. His name is Cambio. Pray,
accept his service.

76

82

BAPTISTA A thousand thanks, Signor Gremio. Welcome, good Cambio. [*To Tranio*.] But, gentle sir,
methinks you walk like a stranger. May I be so bold to
know the cause of your coming?

86

TRANIO

Pardon me, sir, the boldness is mine own,
That, being a stranger in this city here,
Do make myself a suitor to your daughter,
Unto Bianca, fair and virtuous.
Nor is your firm resolve unknown to me,
In the preferment of the eldest sister.
This liberty is all that I request,
That upon knowledge of my parentage
I may have welcome 'mongst the rest that woo,
And free access and favor as the rest.
And toward the education of your daughters
I here bestow a simple instrument,
And this small packet of Greek and Latin books.
If you accept them, then their worth is great.
        [*Biondello brings forward the lute and books*.].

97

BAPTISTA

Lucentio is your name? Of whence, I pray?

102

TRANIO

Of Pisa, sir, son to Vincentio.

BAPTISTA

A mighty man of Pisa. By report

104

76 grateful pleasing   **82 Cambio** (In Italian, appropriately, the word
means "change" or "exchange.")   **86 walk like a stranger** keep your
distance, stand apart   **97 favor** leave, permission   **102 Lucentio . . .
name** (Baptista may have learned this information from a note accom-
panying the books and lute.)   **104 report** reputation

I know him well. You are very welcome, sir.
[*To Hortensio.*] Take you the lute, [*To Lucentio*] and you
    the set of books;
You shall go see your pupils presently.   107
Holla, within!

    Enter a Servant.

           Sirrah, lead these gentlemen
To my daughters, and tell them both
These are their tutors. Bid them use them well.
    [*Exit Servant, with Lucentio and Hortensio.*]
We will go walk a little in the orchard,   111
And then to dinner. You are passing welcome,   112
And so I pray you all to think yourselves.

PETRUCHIO
Signor Baptista, my business asketh haste,
And every day I cannot come to woo.
You knew my father well, and in him me,
Left solely heir to all his lands and goods,
Which I have bettered rather than decreased.
Then tell me, if I get your daughter's love,
What dowry shall I have with her to wife?

BAPTISTA
After my death the one half of my lands,
And in possession twenty thousand crowns.   122

PETRUCHIO
And, for that dowry, I'll assure her of
Her widowhood, be it that she survive me,   124
In all my lands and leases whatsoever.
Let specialties be therefore drawn between us,   126
That covenants may be kept on either hand.

BAPTISTA
Ay, when the special thing is well obtained,
That is, her love; for that is all in all.

PETRUCHIO
· Why, that is nothing, for I tell you, Father,
I am as peremptory as she proud-minded;
And where two raging fires meet together,

---

107 presently immediately   **111 orchard** garden · **112 passing** exceed-
ingly   **122 in possession** i.e., in immediate possession   **124 widowhood**
i.e., widow's share of the estate   **126 specialties** terms of contract

They do consume the thing that feeds their fury.
Though little fire grows great with little wind,
Yet extreme gusts will blow out fire and all.
So I to her, and so she yields to me,
For I am rough and woo not like a babe.

BAPTISTA
Well mayst thou woo, and happy be thy speed!
But be thou armed for some unhappy words.

PETRUCHIO
Ay, to the proof, as mountains are for winds,   140
That shakes not, though they blow perpetually.   141

Enter Hortensio [as Litio], with his head broke.

BAPTISTA
How now, my friend, why dost thou look so pale?

HORTENSIO
For fear, I promise you, if I look pale.

BAPTISTA
What, will my daughter prove a good musician?

HORTENSIO
I think she'll sooner prove a soldier.
Iron may hold with her, but never lutes.   146

BAPTISTA
Why, then thou canst not break her to the lute?   147

HORTENSIO
Why, no, for she hath broke the lute to me.
I did but tell her she mistook her frets,   149
And bowed her hand to teach her fingering,
When, with a most impatient devilish spirit,
"Frets, call you these?" quoth she, "I'll fume with them."
And with that word she struck me on the head,
And through the instrument my pate made way;
And there I stood amazèd for a while,
As on a pillory, looking through the lute,   156

___

140 **to the proof** i.e., in armor, proof against her shrewishness
141 **shakes** shake. **s.d. broke** i.e., with a bleeding cut. (Hortensio
usually appears on stage with his head emerging through a broken
lute.) 146 **hold with** hold out against 147 **break** train (with pun in the
next line) 149 **frets** ridges or bars on the fingerboard of the lute. (But
Kate puns on the sense of "fume," "be indignant.") 156 **pillory**
wooden collar used as punishment

While she did call me rascal fiddler
And twangling Jack, with twenty such vile terms,   158
As had she studied to misuse me so.

PETRUCHIO

Now, by the world, it is a lusty wench!   160
I love her ten times more than e'er I did.
O, how I long to have some chat with her!

BAPTISTA [*To Hortensio*]

Well, go with me and be not so discomfited.
Proceed in practice with my younger daughter;   164
She's apt to learn and thankful for good turns.—
Signor Petruchio, will you go with us,
Or shall I send my daughter Kate to you?

PETRUCHIO

I pray you, do.   *Exeunt. Manet Petruchio.*
                      I'll attend her here,   168
And woo her with some spirit when she comes.
Say that she rail, why then I'll tell her plain
She sings as sweetly as a nightingale.
Say that she frown, I'll say she looks as clear
As morning roses newly washed with dew.
Say she be mute and will not speak a word,
Then I'll commend her volubility
And say she uttereth piercing eloquence.
If she do bid me pack, I'll give her thanks,   177
As though she bid me stay by her a week.
If she deny to wed, I'll crave the day   179
When I shall ask the banns and when be married.   180
But here she comes; and now, Petruchio, speak.

        Enter Katharina.

Good morrow, Kate, for that's your name, I hear.

KATHARINA

Well have you heard, but something hard of hearing.   183
They call me Katharine that do talk of me.

PETRUCHIO

You lie, in faith, for you are called plain Kate,

---

158 Jack knave   **160 lusty** lively   **164 practice** instruction   **168 s.d.**
Manet he remains onstage   **177 pack** begone   **179 deny** refuse   **180 ask**
the banns have a reading of the required announcement in church of a
forthcoming marriage   **183 heard, hard** (Pronounced nearly alike.)

And bonny Kate and sometimes Kate the curst;
But Kate, the prettiest Kate in Christendom,
Kate of Kate Hall, my superdainty Kate,
For dainties are all Kates, and therefore, Kate,   189
Take this of me, Kate of my consolation: 190
Hearing thy mildness praised in every town,
Thy virtues spoke of, and thy beauty sounded,   192
Yet not so deeply as to thee belongs,
Myself am moved to woo thee for my wife.

KATHARINA
Moved? In good time! Let him that moved you hither   195
Remove you hence. I knew you at the first
You were a movable.

PETRUCHIO   Why, what's a movable?   197

KATHARINA
A joint stool.

PETRUCHIO   Thou hast hit it. Come, sit on me.   198

KATHARINA
Asses are made to bear, and so are you.   199

PETRUCHIO
Women are made to bear, and so are you.

KATHARINA
No such jade as you, if me you mean.   201

PETRUCHIO
Alas, good Kate, I will not burden thee,
For knowing thee to be but young and light.   203

KATHARINA
Too light for such a swain as you to catch,   204
And yet as heavy as my weight should be.

PETRUCHIO
Should be? Should—buzz!   206

---

189 all Kates (with a quibble on *cates*, confections, delicacies)   **190 of
me** from me   **192 sounded** proclaimed (with a quibble on "plumbed,"
as indicated by *deeply* in the next line)   **195 In good time** forsooth,
indeed   **197 movable** (1) one easily changed or dissuaded (2) an article
of furniture   **198 joint stool** a well-fitted stool made by an expert
craftsman   **199 bear** carry (with puns in the following lines suggesting
"bear children" and "support a man during sexual intercourse")
201 jade an ill-conditioned horse   **203 light** (1) of delicate stature
(2) lascivious (3) lacking a *burden* (see previous line) in the musical
sense of lacking a bass undersong or accompaniment (4) elusive (in the
following line)   **204 swain** young rustic in love   **206 buzz** i.e., a bee
(punning on *be*) should make a buzzing sound; also, an interjection
expressing impatience or contempt.

KATHARINA   Well ta'en, and like a buzzard. 206

PETRUCHIO
  O slow-winged turtle, shall a buzzard take thee?

KATHARINA
  Ay, for a turtle, as he takes a buzzard.

PETRUCHIO
  Come, come, you wasp, i' faith, you are too angry.   209

KATHARINA
  If I be waspish, best beware my sting.

PETRUCHIO
  My remedy is then to pluck it out.

KATHARINA
  Ay, if the fool could find it where it lies.

PETRUCHIO
  Who knows not where a wasp does wear his sting?
  In his tail.

KATHARINA   In his tongue.

PETRUCHIO   Whose tongue?

KATHARINA
  Yours, if you talk of tails, and so farewell.   217

PETRUCHIO
  What, with my tongue in your tail? Nay, come again.
  Good Kate, I am a gentleman—

KATHARINA   That I'll try. *She strikes him.*

PETRUCHIO
  I swear I'll cuff you, if you strike again.

KATHARINA   So may you lose your arms.
  If you strike me, you are no gentleman,
  And if no gentleman, why then no arms.   223

PETRUCHIO
  A herald, Kate? O, put me in thy books!   224

KATHARINA   What is your crest, a coxcomb?   225

---

206 buzzard (1) figuratively, a fool (2) in the next line, an inferior kind of
hawk, fit only to overtake a slow-winged *turtle* or turtledove, as Petruchio might overtake Kate (3) a buzzing insect, caught by a turtle
209 wasp i.e., waspish, scolding woman (but suggested by *buzzard,*
buzzing insect)   **217 talk of tails** i.e., idly tells stories (with pun on *tale,*
tail)   **223 no arms** no coat of arms (with pun on *arms* as limbs of the
body)   **224 books** (1) books of heraldry, heraldic registers (2) grace,
favor   **225 crest** (1) armorial device (2) a rooster's comb, setting up the
joke on *coxcomb,* the cap of the court fool

PETRUCHIO
  A combless cock, so Kate will be my hen.

KATHARINA
  No cock of mine; you crow too like a craven.   227

PETRUCHIO
  Nay, come, Kate, come, you must not look so sour.

KATHARINA
  It is my fashion when I see a crab.   229

PETRUCHIO
  Why, here's no crab, and therefore look not sour.

KATHARINA There is, there is.

PETRUCHIO
  Then show it me.

KATHARINA   Had I a glass, I would.

PETRUCHIO What, you mean my face?

KATHARINA Well aimed of such a young one.   234

PETRUCHIO
  Now, by Saint George, I am too young for you.

KATHARINA
  Yet you are withered.

PETRUCHIO   'Tis with cares.

KATHARINA   I care not.

PETRUCHIO
  Nay, hear you, Kate. In sooth, you scape not so.

KATHARINA
  I chafe you if I tarry. Let me go.

PETRUCHIO
  No, not a whit. I find you passing gentle.
  'Twas told me you were rough and coy and sullen,   240
  And now I find report a very liar,
  For thou art pleasant, gamesome, passing courteous,   242
  But slow in speech, yet sweet as springtime flowers.   243
  Thou canst not frown, thou canst not look askance,   244
  Nor bite the lip, as angry wenches will,
  Nor hast thou pleasure to be cross in talk;
  But thou with mildness entertain'st thy wooers,
  With gentle conference, soft and affable.

---

227 craven a cock that is not "game" or willing to fight   **229 crab** crab apple   **234 aimed of** guessed for.   **young** i.e., inexperienced. (But Petruchio picks up the word in the sense of "strong.")   **240 coy** disdainful   **242 gamesome** playful, spirited   **243 But slow** never anything but slow   **244 askance** scornfully

Why does the world report that Kate doth limp?
O slanderous world! Kate like the hazel twig
Is straight and slender, and as brown in hue
As hazelnuts, and sweeter than the kernels.
O, let me see thee walk. Thou dost not halt.   253

KATHARINA
Go, fool, and whom thou keep'st command.   254

PETRUCHIO
Did ever Dian so become a grove   255
As Kate this chamber with her princely gait?
O, be thou Dian, and let her be Kate,
And then let Kate be chaste and Dian sportful!   258

KATHARINA
Where did you study all this goodly speech?

PETRUCHIO
It is extempore, from my mother wit.   260

KATHARINA
A witty mother! Witless else her son.   261

PETRUCHIO   Am I not wise?   262

KATHARINA   Yes, keep you warm.   263

PETRUCHIO
Marry, so I mean, sweet Katharine, in thy bed.
And therefore, setting all this chat aside,
Thus in plain terms: your father hath consented
That you shall be my wife; your dowry 'greed on;
And, will you, nill you, I will marry you.   268
Now, Kate, I am a husband for your turn,   269
For by this light, whereby I see thy beauty—
Thy beauty that doth make me like thee well—
Thou must be married to no man but me;

> *Enter Baptista, Gremio, [and] Tranio [as Lucentio].*

For I am he am born to tame you, Kate,

---

253 halt limp   **254 whom thou keep'st** i.e., those whom you employ,
your servants   **255 Dian** Diana, goddess of the hunt and of chastity.
become adorn   **258 sportful** amorous   **260 mother wit** native intelligence   **261 Witless . . . son** i.e., without the intelligence inherited from
her, he would have none at all   **262–263 wise . . . warm** (An allusion to
the proverbial phrase "enough wit to keep oneself warm.")   **268 nill
you** will you not   **269 for your turn** to suit you

And bring you from a wild Kate to a Kate   274
Conformable as other household Kates.
Here comes your father. Never make denial;
I must and will have Katharine to my wife.

BAPTISTA
Now, Signor Petruchio, how speed you with my
  daughter?

PETRUCHIO
How but well, sir, how but well?
It were impossible I should speed amiss.   280

BAPTISTA
Why, how now, daughter Katharine, in your dumps?

KATHARINA
Call you me daughter? Now, I promise you,   282
You have showed a tender fatherly regard,
To wish me wed to one half lunatic,
A madcap ruffian and a swearing Jack,
That thinks with oaths to face the matter out.   286

PETRUCHIO
Father, 'tis thus: yourself and all the world,
That talked of her, have talked amiss of her.
If she be curst, it is for policy,   289
For she's not froward, but modest as the dove.   290
She is not hot, but temperate as the morn.
For patience she will prove a second Grissel,   292
And Roman Lucrece for her chastity.   293
And to conclude, we have 'greed so well together
That upon Sunday is the wedding day.

KATHARINA
I'll see thee hanged on Sunday first.

GREMIO Hark, Petruchio, she says she'll see thee hanged
  first.

TRANIO
Is this your speeding? Nay then, good night our part!

---

274 wild Kate (with a quibble on *wildcat*)   **280 speed** fare, get on
282 promise assure   **286 face** brazen   **289 policy** cunning, ulterior
motive   **290 froward** willful, perverse   **292 Grissel** patient Griselda, the
epitome of wifely patience and devotion (whose story was told by
Chaucer in "The Clerk's Tale" of *The Canterbury Tales* and earlier by
Boccaccio and Petrarch)   **293 Roman Lucrece** Lucretia, a Roman lady
who took her own life after her chastity had been violated by the Tar-
quin prince, Sextus. (Shakespeare told the story in *The Rape of Lucrece*.)

PETRUCHIO
　Be patient, gentlemen, I choose her for myself.
　If she and I be pleased, what's that to you?
　'Tis bargained twixt us twain, being alone,
　That she shall still be curst in company.
　I tell you, 'tis incredible to believe
　How much she loves me. O, the kindest Kate!
　She hung about my neck, and kiss on kiss
　She vied so fast, protesting oath on oath,   307
　That in a twink she won me to her love.
　O, you are novices! 'Tis a world to see   309
　How tame, when men and women are alone,
　A meacock wretch can make the curstest shrew.—   311
　Give me thy hand, Kate. I will unto Venice
　To buy apparel 'gainst the wedding day.—   313
　Provide the feast, Father, and bid the guests;
　I will be sure my Katharine shall be fine.   315
BAPTISTA
　I know not what to say. But give me your hands.
　God send you joy, Petruchio! 'Tis a match.
GREMIO, TRANIO
　Amen, say we. We will be witnesses.
PETRUCHIO
　Father, and wife, and gentlemen, adieu.
　I will to Venice. Sunday comes apace.
　We will have rings and things, and fine array;
　And kiss me, Kate, we will be married o' Sunday.   322
　　　　Exeunt Petruchio and Katharine [separately].
GREMIO
　Was ever match clapped up so suddenly?   323
BAPTISTA
　Faith, gentlemen, now I play a merchant's part,
　And venture madly on a desperate mart.   325
TRANIO
　'Twas a commodity lay fretting by you;   326
　'Twill bring you gain, or perish on the seas.

307 vied went me one better, kiss for kiss　**309 a world** worth a whole
world　**311 meacock** cowardly　**313 'gainst** in anticipation of　**315 fine**
elegantly dressed　**322 kiss me** (Petruchio probably kisses her.)
323 clapped up settled (by a shaking of hands)　**325 desperate mart**
risky venture　**326 lay fretting** i.e., which lay in storage being destroyed
by moths, weevils, or spoilage (with a pun on "chafing")

BAPTISTA
    The gain I seek is quiet in the match.

GREMIO
    No doubt but he hath got a quiet catch.   329
    But now, Baptista, to your younger daughter.
    Now is the day we long have lookèd for.
    I am your neighbor, and was suitor first.

TRANIO
    And I am one that love Bianca more
    Than words can witness or your thoughts can guess.

GREMIO
    Youngling, thou canst not love so dear as I.

TRANIO
    Graybeard, thy love doth freeze.

GREMIO   But thine doth fry.
    Skipper, stand back. 'Tis age that nourisheth.   337

TRANIO
    But youth in ladies' eyes that flourisheth.

BAPTISTA
    Content you, gentlemen. I will compound this strife.   339
    'Tis deeds must win the prize, and he of both   340
    That can assure my daughter greatest dower
    Shall have my Bianca's love.
    Say, Signor Gremio, what can you assure her?

GREMIO
    First, as you know, my house within the city
    Is richly furnishèd with plate and gold,
    Basins and ewers to lave her dainty hands;   346
    My hangings all of Tyrian tapestry;   347
    In ivory coffers I have stuffed my crowns;
    In cypress chests my arras counterpoints,   349
    Costly apparel, tents, and canopies,   350
    Fine linen, Turkey cushions bossed with pearl,   351
    Valance of Venice gold in needlework,   352
    Pewter and brass, and all things that belongs
    To house or housekeeping. Then at my farm

---

329 quiet catch (Said ironically; Gremio is sure that Kate will be anything but quiet.)   **337 Skipper** flighty fellow   **339 compound** settle   **340 he of both** i.e., the one of you two   **346 lave** wash   **347 Tyrian** dark red or purple   **349 arras counterpoints** counterpanes of tapestry   **350 tents** bed-curtains   **351 Turkey** Turkish.   **bossed** embossed   **352 Valance** drapery around the canopy or bed frame

I have a hundred milch kine to the pail,   355
Sixscore fat oxen standing in my stalls,
And all things answerable to this portion.   357
Myself am struck in years, I must confess,   358
And if I die tomorrow, this is hers,
If whilst I live she will be only mine.

TRANIO
That "only" came well in. Sir, list to me:
I am my father's heir and only son.
If I may have your daughter to my wife,
I'll leave her houses three or four as good,
Within rich Pisa walls, as any one
Old Signor Gremio has in Padua,
Besides two thousand ducats by the year   367
Of fruitful land, all which shall be her jointure.   368
What, have I pinched you, Signor Gremio?

GREMIO
Two thousand ducats by the year of land!
[Aside.] My land amounts not to so much in all.—
That she shall have, besides an argosy   372
That now is lying in Marseilles' road.   373
[To Tranio.] What, have I choked you with an argosy?

TRANIO
Gremio, 'tis known my father hath no less
Than three great argosies, besides two galliases   376
And twelve tight galleys. These I will assure her,   377
And twice as much, whate'er thou offerest next.

GREMIO
Nay, I have offered all. I have no more,
And she can have no more than all I have.
[To Baptista.] If you like me, she shall have me and mine.

TRANIO
Why, then the maid is mine from all the world,
By your firm promise. Gremio is outvied.

BAPTISTA
I must confess your offer is the best;

355 **milch kine to the pail** dairy cattle   357 **answerable to** on the same
scale as   358 **struck** advanced   367 **ducats** gold coins   368 **Of** from.
jointure marriage settlement   372 **argosy** merchant vessel of the largest
size   373 **road** roadstead, harbor   376 **galliases** heavy, low-built vessels   377 **tight** watertight

And, let your father make her the assurance,   · 385
She is your own; else, you must pardon me.
If you should die before him, where's her dower?

TRANIO
That's but a cavil. He is old, I young.

GREMIO
And may not young men die as well as old?

BAPTISTA
Well, gentlemen, I am thus resolved:
On Sunday next, you know
My daughter Katharine is to be married.
Now on the Sunday following shall Bianca
Be bride [*To Tranio*] to you, if you make this assurance;
If not, to Signor Gremio.
And so I take my leave, and thank you both.   *Exit.*

GREMIO
Adieu, good neighbor.—Now I fear thee not.
Sirrah young gamester, your father were a fool
To give thee all, and in his waning age
Set foot under thy table. Tut, a toy!   400
An old Italian fox is not so kind, my boy.   *Exit.*

TRANIO
A vengeance on your crafty withered hide!
Yet I have faced it with a card of ten.   403
'Tis in my head to do my master good.
I see no reason but supposed Lucentio
Must get a father, called supposed Vincentio,
And that's a wonder. Fathers commonly
Do get their children; but in this case of wooing,   408
A child shall get a sire, if I fail not of my cunning.
                                                 Exit.

✤

---

385 let provided   **400 Set . . . table** i.e., become a dependent in your
household.   **a toy** nonsense   **403 faced . . . ten** brazened it out with only
a ten-spot of cards   **408 get** beget (with a play on *get*, obtain, in l. 406)

3.1   *Enter Lucentio [as Cambio], Hortensio [as Litio], and Bianca.*

LUCENTIO

Fiddler, forbear. You grow too forward, sir.
Have you so soon forgot the entertainment
Her sister Katharine welcomed you withal?

HORTENSIO

But, wrangling pedant, this is
The patroness of heavenly harmony.
Then give me leave to have prerogative,   6
And when in music we have spent an hour
Your lecture shall have leisure for as much.   8

LUCENTIO

Preposterous ass, that never read so far   9
To know the cause why music was ordained!
Was it not to refresh the mind of man
After his studies or his usual pain?   12
Then give me leave to read philosophy,
And, while I pause, serve in your harmony.   14

HORTENSIO

Sirrah, I will not bear these braves of thine.   15

BIANCA

Why, gentlemen, you do me double wrong
To strive for that which resteth in my choice.
I am no breeching scholar in the schools;   18
I'll not be tied to hours nor 'pointed times,
But learn my lessons as I please myself.
And, to cut off all strife, here sit we down.
[*To Hortensio.*] Take you your instrument, play you the
     whiles;
His lecture will be done ere you have tuned.

HORTENSIO

You'll leave his lecture when I am in tune?

LUCENTIO

That will be never. Tune your instrument.
                    [*Hortensio moves aside and tunes.*]

3.1. Location: The same.
6 prerogative precedence   **8 lecture** lesson   **9 Preposterous** inverting
the natural order of things, unreasonable   **12 pain** labor   **14 serve in**
present, serve up   **15 braves** insults   **18 breeching scholar** i.e., school-
boy liable to be whipped

BIANCA   Where left we last?

LUCENTIO   Here, madam. [*Reads.*]
 "Hic ibat Simois; hic est Sigeia tellus;   28
 Hic steterat Priami regia celsa senis."   29

BIANCA   Conster them.   30

LUCENTIO   *"Hic ibat,"* as I told you before, *"Simois,"* I
am Lucentio, *"hic est,"* son unto Vincentio of Pisa,
"Sigeia tellus," disguised thus to get your love; *"Hic
steterat,"* and that Lucentio that comes a-wooing,
"Priami," is my man Tranio, *"regia,"* bearing my port,   35
"celsa senis," that we might beguile the old panta-   36
loon.   37

HORTENSIO   Madam, my instrument's in tune.

BIANCA   Let's hear. [*He plays.*] O fie! The treble jars.

LUCENTIO   Spit in the hole, man, and tune again.   40
          [*Hortensio moves aside.*]

BIANCA   Now let me see if I can conster it: *"Hic ibat Simois,"* I know you not, *"hic est Sigeia tellus,"* I trust
you not; *"Hic steterat Priami,"* take heed he hear us
not, *"regia,"* presume not, *"celsa senis,"* despair not.

HORTENSIO
Madam, 'tis now in tune.   [*He plays again.*]

LUCENTIO   All but the bass.

HORTENSIO
The bass is right; 'tis the base knave that jars.
[*Aside.*] How fiery and forward our pedant is!
Now, for my life, the knave doth court my love.
Pedascule, I'll watch you better yet.   49

BIANCA [*To Lucentio*]
In time I may believe, yet I mistrust.

LUCENTIO
Mistrust it not, for, sure, Aeacides   51
Was Ajax, called so from his grandfather.

28–29 Hic . . . senis here flowed the river Simois; here is the Sigeian
land; here stood the lofty palace of old Priam. (Ovid, *Heroides*,
1.33–34.)   **30 Conster** construe   **35 port** social position, style of
living   **36–37 pantaloon** foolish old man, i.e., Gremio   **40 Spit in the
hole** i.e., to make the peg stick   **49 Pedascule** (A word contemptuously
coined by Hortensio, the vocative of *pedasculus*, little pedant.)
51 Aeacides descendant of Aeacus, King of Aegina, father of Telamon
and grandfather of Ajax. (Lucentio is pretending to go on with his
lesson.)

BIANCA
    I must believe my master; else, I promise you,
    I should be arguing still upon that doubt.
    But let it rest.—Now, Litio, to you:
    Good master, take it not unkindly, pray,
    That I have been thus pleasant with you both.   57
HORTENSIO [*To Lucentio*]
    You may go walk, and give me leave awhile.
    My lessons make no music in three parts.
LUCENTIO
    Are you so formal, sir? Well, I must wait,   60
    [*Aside*] And watch withal; for, but I be deceived,   61
    Our fine musician groweth amorous.
                                        [*He moves aside.*]
HORTENSIO
    Madam, before you touch the instrument,
    To learn the order of my fingering,   64
    I must begin with rudiments of art,
    To teach you gamut in a briefer sort,   66
    More pleasant, pithy, and effectual
    Than hath been taught by any of my trade.
    And there it is in writing, fairly drawn.   69
                                        [*He gives her a paper.*]
BIANCA
    Why, I am past my gamut long ago.
HORTENSIO
    Yet read the gamut of Hortensio.
BIANCA [*Reads*]
    "*Gamut* I am, the ground of all accord,   72
    A re, to plead Hortensio's passion;
    B mi, Bianca, take him for thy lord,
    C fa ut, that loves with all affection.   75
    D sol re, one clef, two notes have I;
    E la mi, show pity, or I die."

57 **pleasant** merry   60 **formal** precise   61 **but** unless   64 **order**
method   66 **gamut** the scale, from the alphabet name (*gamma*) of the
first note plus *ut*, its syllable name, now commonly called *do*. (The
gamut of Hortensio begins on G instead of on C.)   69 **drawn** set out,
copied   72 **ground** bass note, foundation.   **accord** harmony   75 **fa ut**
(The note C is the fourth note, or *fa*, of a scale based on G, but is the
first note, *ut*, or *do*, of the more universal major scale based on C.
Similarly, D is fifth note or *sol* in the G scale but second or *re* in the C
scale; similarly with E as sixth and third.)

Call you this gamut? Tut, I like it not.
Old fashions please me best; I am not so nice   79
To change true rules for odd inventions.

    Enter a [Servant as] messenger.

SERVANT
Mistress, your father prays you leave your books
And help to dress your sister's chamber up.
You know tomorrow is the wedding day.

BIANCA
Farewell, sweet masters both, I must be gone.
              [Exeunt Bianca and Servant.]

LUCENTIO
Faith, mistress, then I have no cause to stay.   *[Exit.]*

HORTENSIO
But I have cause to pry into this pedant.
Methinks he looks as though he were in love.
Yet if thy thoughts, Bianca, be so humble
To cast thy wandering eyes on every stale,   89
Seize thee that list. If once I find thee ranging,   90
Hortensio will be quit with thee by changing.   *Exit.* 91

                        ❖

3.2   *Enter Baptista, Gremio, Tranio [as Lucentio],*
       Katharine, Bianca, [Lucentio as Cambio], and
       others, attendants.

BAPTISTA *[To Tranio]*
Signor Lucentio, this is the 'pointed day
That Katharine and Petruchio should be married,
And yet we hear not of our son-in-law.
What will be said? What mockery will it be,
To want the bridegroom when the priest attends   5
To speak the ceremonial rites of marriage?
What says Lucentio to this shame of ours?

79 nice capricious   **89 stale** decoy, bait   **90 Seize . . . list** let him who
wants you have you.   **ranging** inconstant   **91 be quit** get even.   **changing** i.e., loving another

3.2. Location: Padua. Before Baptista's house.
5 want lack

KATHARINA

No shame but mine. I must, forsooth, be forced
To give my hand opposed against my heart
Unto a mad-brain rudesby full of spleen,   10
Who wooed in haste and means to wed at leisure.
I told you, I, he was a frantic fool,
Hiding his bitter jests in blunt behavior.
And, to be noted for a merry man,
He'll woo a thousand, 'point the day of marriage,
Make friends, invite, and proclaim the banns,
Yet never means to wed where he hath wooed.
Now must the world point at poor Katharine
And say, "Lo, there is mad Petruchio's wife,
If it would please him come and marry her!"

TRANIO

Patience, good Katharine, and Baptista too.
Upon my life, Petruchio means but well,
Whatever fortune stays him from his word.
Though he be blunt, I know him passing wise;
Though he be merry, yet withal he's honest.

KATHARINA

Would Katharine had never seen him though!

Exit weeping.

BAPTISTA

Go, girl, I cannot blame thee now to weep,
For such an injury would vex a very saint,
Much more a shrew of thy impatient humor.

Enter Biondello.

BIONDELLO Master, master! News, and such old news 30
as you never heard of!

BAPTISTA Is it new and old too? How may that be?

BIONDELLO Why, is it not news to hear of Petruchio's
coming?

BAPTISTA Is he come?

BIONDELLO Why, no, sir.

BAPTISTA What, then?

BIONDELLO He is coming.

BAPTISTA When will he be here?

---

10 rudesby unmannerly fellow. **spleen** i.e., changeable temper **30 old**
rare; or perhaps referring to Petruchio's old clothes

BIONDELLO   When he stands where I am and sees you
there.

TRANIO   But say, what to thine old news?   42

BIONDELLO   Why, Petruchio is coming in a new hat and
an old jerkin; a pair of old breeches thrice turned; a   44
pair of boots that have been candle-cases, one buck-   45
led, another laced; an old rusty sword ta'en out of the
town armory, with a broken hilt, and chapeless; with   47
two broken points; his horse hipped, with an old   48
mothy saddle and stirrups of no kindred; besides,
possessed with the glanders and like to mose in the   50
chine, troubled with the lampass, infected with the   51
fashions, full of windgalls, sped with spavins, rayed   52
with the yellows, past cure of the fives, stark spoiled   53
with the staggers, begnawn with the bots, swayed in   54
the back and shoulder-shotten; near-legged before;   55
and with a half-cheeked bit and a headstall of sheep's   56
leather which, being restrained to keep him from   57
stumbling, hath been often burst and now repaired
with knots; one girth six times pieced, and a woman's   59

---

42 to about   **44 jerkin** man's jacket.   **turned** i.e., with the material
reversed to get more wear   **45 candle-cases** i.e., discarded boots, used
only as a receptacle for candle ends   **47 chapeless** without the chape,
the metal plate or mounting of a scabbard, especially that which covers
the point   **48 points** tagged laces for attaching hose to doublet.   **hipped**
lamed in the hip. (Almost all the diseases here named are described in
Gervase Markham's *How to Choose, Ride, Train, and Diet both Hunting
Horses and Running Horses . . . Also a Discourse of Horsemanship,*
probably first published in 1593.)   **50 glanders** contagious disease in
horses causing swelling beneath the jaw and mucous discharge from
the nostrils   **50–51 mose in the chine** suffer from glanders   **51 lampass**
a thick spongy flesh growing over a horse's upper teeth and hindering
his eating   **52 fashions** i.e., farcins, or farcy, a disease like glanders.
windgalls soft tumors or swellings generally found on the fetlock joint,
so called from having been supposed to contain air.   **sped** far gone.
spavins a disease of the hock, marked by a small bony enlargement
inside the leg.   **rayed** defiled   **53 yellows** jaundice.   **fives** avives, a
glandular disease causing swelling behind the ear   **54 staggers** a
disease causing palsylike staggering.   **bots** parasitic worms
55 shoulder-shotten with sprained or dislocated shoulder.   **near-legged
before** with knock-kneed forelegs   **56 half-cheeked bit** one to which the
bridle is attached halfway up the cheek or sidepiece and thus not giving
sufficient control over the horse.   **headstall** part of the bridle over the
head   **56–57 sheep's leather** (i.e., of inferior quality; pigskin was used
for strongest harness)   **57 restrained** drawn back   **59 pieced** mended

crupper of velour, which hath two letters for her name 60
fairly set down in studs, and here and there pieced
with packthread.

BAPTISTA   Who comes with him?

BIONDELLO   O, sir, his lackey, for all the world capari- 64
soned like the horse; with a linen stock on one leg and 65
a kersey boot-hose on the other, gartered with a red 66
and blue list; an old hat, and the humor of forty fancies 67
pricked in 't for a feather—a monster, a very monster 68
in apparel, and not like a Christian footboy or a gentleman's lackey.

TRANIO
'Tis some odd humor pricks him to this fashion;   71
Yet oftentimes he goes but mean-appareled.

BAPTISTA   I am glad he's come, howsoe'er he comes.

BIONDELLO   Why, sir, he comes not.

BAPTISTA   Didst thou not say he comes?

BIONDELLO   Who? That Petruchio came?

BAPTISTA   Ay, that Petruchio came.

BIONDELLO   No, sir, I say his horse comes, with him on
his back.

BAPTISTA   Why, that's all one.   80

BIONDELLO
    Nay, by Saint Jamy,
    I hold you a penny,   82
    A horse and a man
    Is more than one,
    And yet not many.

    Enter Petruchio and Grumio.

PETRUCHIO
    Come, where be these gallants? Who's at home?

BAPTISTA   You are welcome, sir.

PETRUCHIO   And yet I come not well.

BAPTISTA   And yet you halt not.   89

---

60 crupper leather loop passing under the horse's tail and fastened to
the saddle.   **velour** velvet   **64–65 caparisoned** outfitted   **65 stock**
stocking   **66 kersey boot-hose** overstocking of coarse material for
wearing under boots   **67 list** strip of cloth.   **the humor . . . fancies** i.e.,
with a caprice equal to some forty imaginings (?)   **68 pricked** pinned
71 humor pricks whim that spurs   **80 all one** the same thing   **82 hold**
wager   **89 halt** limp, move slowly

TRANIO
Not so well appareled as I wish you were.

PETRUCHIO
Were it better, I should rush in thus. 91
But where is Kate? Where is my lovely bride?
How does my father? Gentles, methinks you frown.
And wherefore gaze this goodly company
As if they saw some wondrous monument, 95
Some comet, or unusual prodigy? 96

BAPTISTA
Why, sir, you know this is your wedding day.
First were we sad, fearing you would not come,
Now sadder that you come so unprovided. 99
Fie, doff this habit, shame to your estate, 100
An eyesore to our solemn festival!

TRANIO
And tell us what occasion of import
Hath all so long detained you from your wife
And sent you hither so unlike yourself?

PETRUCHIO
Tedious it were to tell, and harsh to hear.
Sufficeth I am come to keep my word,
Though in some part enforcèd to digress, 107
Which at more leisure I will so excuse
As you shall well be satisfied withal.
But where is Kate? I stay too long from her.
The morning wears; 'tis time we were at church.

TRANIO
See not your bride in these unreverent robes.
Go to my chamber; put on clothes of mine.

PETRUCHIO
Not I, believe me. Thus I'll visit her.

BAPTISTA
But thus, I trust, you will not marry her.

PETRUCHIO
Good sooth, even thus. Therefore ha' done with words.
To me she's married, not unto my clothes.

---

91 Were it even if it (my apparel) were. **rush** come quickly (referring to
halt not in l. 89) **95 monument** portent **96 prodigy** omen **99 unprovided** ill equipped **100 estate** position, station **107 digress** i.e., deviate
from my promise

Could I repair what she will wear in me   118
As I can change these poor accoutrements,
'Twere well for Kate and better for myself.
But what a fool am I to chat with you,
When I should bid good morrow to my bride
And seal the title with a lovely kiss!   *Exit.* 123

TRANIO
He hath some meaning in his mad attire.
We will persuade him, be it possible,
To put on better ere he go to church.

BAPTISTA
I'll after him and see the event of this.   127
                    Exit [with all but Tranio and Lucentio].

TRANIO
But, sir, love concerneth us to add   128
Her father's liking, which to bring to pass,   129
As I before imparted to your worship,
I am to get a man—whate'er he be
It skills not much, we'll fit him to our turn—   132
And he shall be Vincentio of Pisa,
And make assurance here in Padua
Of greater sums than I have promisèd.
So shall you quietly enjoy your hope
And marry sweet Bianca with consent.

LUCENTIO
Were it not that my fellow schoolmaster
Doth watch Bianca's steps so narrowly,
'Twere good, methinks, to steal our marriage,   140
Which once performed, let all the world say no,
I'll keep mine own, despite of all the world.

TRANIO
That by degrees we mean to look into,
And watch our vantage in this business.   144
We'll overreach the graybeard, Gremio,
The narrow-prying father, Minola,   146

118 Could . . . me if I could amend in my character what she'll have to
put up with   123 lovely loving   127 event outcome   128–129 love . . .
liking i.e., our love plot to secure Bianca makes it our business to
secure Baptista's approval of the feigned "Lucentio" as wooer
132 skills matters   140 steal our marriage i.e., elope   144 vantage
opportunity, advantage   146 narrow-prying suspicious, watchful

The quaint musician, amorous Litio,   147
All for my master's sake, Lucentio.

    Enter Gremio.

Signor Gremio, came you from the church?

GREMIO
As willingly as e'er I came from school.

TRANIO
And is the bride and bridegroom coming home?

GREMIO
A bridegroom, say you? 'Tis a groom indeed,   152
A grumbling groom, and that the girl shall find.

TRANIO
Curster than she? Why, 'tis impossible.

GREMIO
Why, he's a devil, a devil, a very fiend.

TRANIO
Why, she's a devil, a devil, the devil's dam.   156

GREMIO
Tut, she's a lamb, a dove, a fool to him.   157
I'll tell you, Sir Lucentio. When the priest
Should ask if Katharine should be his wife,
"Ay, by gogs wouns," quoth he, and swore so loud   160
That all amazed the priest let fall the book,
And as he stooped again to take it up,
This mad-brained bridegroom took him such a cuff   163
That down fell priest and book, and book and priest.
"Now take them up," quoth he, "if any list."   165

TRANIO
What said the wench when he rose again?

GREMIO
Trembled and shook, forwhy he stamped and swore   167
As if the vicar meant to cozen him.   168
But after many ceremonies done,
He calls for wine. "A health!" quoth he, as if
He had been aboard, carousing to his mates   171

---

147 quaint skillful   152 a groom indeed i.e., a fine bridegroom he is.
(Said ironically, with pun on the sense of "servant," "rough fellow.")
156 dam mother   157 a fool to i.e., a pitiable weak creature compared
with   160 gogs wouns God's (Christ's) wounds   163 took gave, struck
165 list choose   167 forwhy because   168 cozen cheat   171 aboard
aboard ship

After a storm; quaffed off the muscatel
And threw the sops all in the sexton's face,   173
Having no other reason
But that his beard grew thin and hungerly   175
And seemed to ask him sops as he was drinking.
This done, he took the bride about the neck
And kissed her lips with such a clamorous smack
That at the parting all the church did echo.
And I seeing this came thence for very shame,
And after me, I know, the rout is coming.   181
Such a mad marriage never was before.
Hark, hark! I hear the minstrels play.   *Music plays.*

Enter Petruchio, Kate, Bianca, Hortensio [as
Litio], Baptista [with Grumio, and train].

PETRUCHIO
Gentlemen and friends, I thank you for your pains.
I know you think to dine with me today,
And have prepared great store of wedding cheer,
But so it is my haste doth call me hence,
And therefore here I mean to take my leave.

BAPTISTA
Is 't possible you will away tonight?

PETRUCHIO
I must away today, before night come.
Make it no wonder. If you knew my business,   191
You would entreat me rather go than stay.
And, honest company, I thank you all   193
That have beheld me give away myself
To this most patient, sweet, and virtuous wife.
Dine with my father, drink a health to me,
For I must hence; and farewell to you all.

TRANIO
Let us entreat you stay till after dinner.

PETRUCHIO
It may not be.

GREMIO   Let me entreat you.

PETRUCHIO
It cannot be.

---

173 sops cakes or bread soaked in the wine   **175 hungerly** hungry
looking, having a starved or famished look   **181 rout** crowd, wedding
party   **191 Make** consider   **193 honest** worthy, kind

KATHARINA   Let me entreat you.

PETRUCHIO
  I am content.

KATHARINA   Are you content to stay?

PETRUCHIO
  I am content you shall entreat me stay;
  But yet not stay, entreat me how you can.

KATHARINA
  Now, if you love me, stay.

PETRUCHIO   Grumio, my horse.   204

GRUMIO   Ay, sir, they be ready; the oats have eaten the   205
  horses.   206

KATHARINA   Nay, then,
  Do what thou canst, I will not go today,
  No, nor tomorrow, not till I please myself.
  The door is open, sir, there lies your way;
  You may be jogging whiles your boots are green.   211
  For me, I'll not be gone till I please myself.
  'Tis like you'll prove a jolly surly groom,   213
  That take it on you at the first so roundly.   214

PETRUCHIO
  O Kate, content thee; prithee, be not angry.

KATHARINA
  I will be angry. What hast thou to do?—   216
  Father, be quiet. He shall stay my leisure.   217

GREMIO
  Ay, marry, sir, now it begins to work.   218

KATHARINA
  Gentlemen, forward to the bridal dinner.
  I see a woman may be made a fool
  If she had not a spirit to resist.

PETRUCHIO
  They shall go forward, Kate, at thy command.—
  Obey the bride, you that attend on her.
  Go to the feast, revel and domineer,   224

---

204 horse horses   **205–206 oats . . . horses** (A comic inversion.)   **211 be
. . . green** (Proverbial for "getting an early start," with a sarcastic
allusion to his unseemly attire.)   **green** fresh, new   **213 like** likely.
jolly arrogant, overbearing   **214 take it on you** i.e., throw your weight
around.   **roundly** unceremoniously   **216 What . . . do** i.e., what business is it of yours   **217 stay my leisure** wait until I am ready   **218 it . . .
work** things are starting to happen   **224 domineer** feast riotously

Carouse full measure to her maidenhead,
Be mad and merry, or go hang yourselves.
But for my bonny Kate, she must with me.   227
Nay, look not big, nor stamp, nor stare, nor fret;   228
I will be master of what is mine own.
She is my goods, my chattels; she is my house,
My household stuff, my field, my barn,
My horse, my ox, my ass, my anything;   232
And here she stands, touch her whoever dare.
I'll bring mine action on the proudest he   234
That stops my way in Padua.—Grumio,
Draw forth thy weapon; we are beset with thieves.   236
Rescue thy mistress, if thou be a man.—
Fear not, sweet wench, they shall not touch thee, Kate!
I'll buckler thee against a million.   239
            Exeunt Petruchio, Katharina, [and Grumio].

BAPTISTA
Nay, let them go, a couple of quiet ones.

GREMIO
Went they not quickly, I should die with laughing.

TRANIO
Of all mad matches never was the like.

LUCENTIO
Mistress, what's your opinion of your sister?

BIANCA
That, being mad herself, she's madly mated.

GREMIO
I warrant him, Petruchio is Kated.   245

BAPTISTA
Neighbors and friends, though bride and bridegroom
            wants   246
For to supply the places at the table,   247
You know there wants no junkets at the feast.   248
Lucentio, you shall supply the bridegroom's place,
And let Bianca take her sister's room.

---

227 for as for   **228 big** threatening   **232 ox . . . anything** (This catalogue
of a man's possessions is from the Tenth Commandment.)   **234 action**
(1) lawsuit (2) attack   **236 Draw** (Perhaps Petruchio and Grumio actually
draw their swords.)   **239 buckler** shield, defend   **245 Kated** Gremio's
invention for "mated (and matched) with Kate"   **246 wants** are lacking   **246–247 wants For to supply** are not present to fill   **248 junkets**
sweetmeats

TRANIO
   Shall sweet Bianca practice how to bride it?   251
BAPTISTA
   She shall, Lucentio. Come, gentlemen, let's go.

                                        Exeunt.

❖

---

251 bride it play the bride

4.1 *Enter Grumio.*

GRUMIO Fie, fie on all tired jades, on all mad masters, 1
and all foul ways! Was ever man so beaten? Was ever 2
man so rayed? Was ever man so weary? I am sent be- 3
fore to make a fire, and they are coming after to warm
them. Now, were not I a little pot and soon hot, my 5
very lips might freeze to my teeth, my tongue to the
roof of my mouth, my heart in my belly, ere I should
come by a fire to thaw me. But I, with blowing the
fire, shall warm myself; for, considering the weather,
a taller man than I will take cold. Holla, ho! Curtis! 10

Enter Curtis.

CURTIS Who is that calls so coldly?

GRUMIO A piece of ice. If thou doubt it, thou mayst
slide from my shoulder to my heel with no greater a
run but my head and my neck. A fire, good Curtis.

CURTIS Is my master and his wife coming, Grumio?

GRUMIO O, ay, Curtis, ay, and therefore fire, fire; cast 16
on no water. 17

CURTIS Is she so hot a shrew as she's reported?

GRUMIO She was, good Curtis, before this frost. But,
thou know'st, winter tames man, woman, and beast;
for it hath tamed my old master and my new mistress
and myself, fellow Curtis.

CURTIS Away, you three-inch fool! I am no beast. 23

GRUMIO Am I but three inches? Why, thy horn is a foot, 24
and so long am I at the least. But wilt thou make a fire,
or shall I complain on thee to our mistress, whose
hand, she being now at hand, thou shalt soon feel, to
thy cold comfort, for being slow in thy hot office? 28

4.1. Location: Petruchio's country house. A table is set out, with seats.
1 jades ill-conditioned horses   **2 ways** roads   **3 rayed** dirtied   **5 a little
. . . hot** (Proverbial expression for a person of small stature soon an-
gered.)   **10 taller** (with play on the meaning "better," "finer")
16–17 cast . . . water (Alludes to the round "Scotland's burning," in
which the phrase "Fire, fire!" is followed by "Pour on water, pour on
water.")   **23 three-inch fool** (Another reference to Grumio's size.)   **I am
no beast** (Curtis protests being called *fellow* by Grumio, since Grumio in
his previous speech has paralleled himself with *beast*.)   **24 horn** i.e.,
cuckold's horn   **28 hot office** i.e., duty of providing a fire

CURTIS   I prithee, good Grumio, tell me, how goes the
world?

GRUMIO   A cold world, Curtis, in every office but thine,
and therefore fire. Do thy duty, and have thy duty, for 32
my master and mistress are almost frozen to death.

CURTIS   There's fire ready, and therefore, good Grumio,
the news.

GRUMIO   Why, "Jack boy, ho, boy!" and as much news 36
as wilt thou.

CURTIS   Come, you are so full of coney-catching! 38

GRUMIO   Why, therefore fire, for I have caught extreme
cold. Where's the cook? Is supper ready, the house
trimmed, rushes strewed, cobwebs swept, the serving- 41
men in their new fustian, their white stockings, and 42
every officer his wedding garment on? Be the jacks fair 43
within, the jills fair without, the carpets laid, and 44
everything in order?

CURTIS   All ready; and therefore, I pray thee, news.

GRUMIO   First know my horse is tired, my master and
mistress fallen out.

CURTIS   How?

GRUMIO   Out of their saddles into the dirt—and thereby
hangs a tale.

CURTIS   Let's ha 't, good Grumio.

GRUMIO   Lend thine ear.

CURTIS   Here.

GRUMIO   There.   *[He cuffs Curtis.]*

CURTIS   This 'tis to feel a tale, not to hear a tale.

GRUMIO   And therefore 'tis called a sensible tale, and this 57
cuff was but to knock at your ear and beseech
listening. Now I begin: Imprimis, we came down a foul 59
hill, my master riding behind my mistress—

CURTIS   Both of one horse? 61

GRUMIO   What's that to thee?

---

32 have thy duty receive your reward   **36 Jack . . . boy** (The first
line of another round or catch.)   **38 coney-catching** cheating,
trickery (with a play on *catch*, round, in the previous line)   **41 rushes**
(Used to cover the floor.)   **42 fustian** coarse cloth of cotton and flax
43 officer household servant   **43, 44 jacks, jills** drinking measures
of one-half and one-fourth pints (with quibble on "servingmen" and
"maidservants")   **44 carpets** table covers   **57 sensible** (1) capable of
being felt (2) showing good sense   **59 Imprimis** in the first place.
foul muddy   **61 of** on

CURTIS Why, a horse.

GRUMIO Tell thou the tale. But hadst thou not crossed 64
me, thou shouldst have heard how her horse fell and
she under her horse; thou shouldst have heard in how
miry a place, how she was bemoiled, how he left her 67
with the horse upon her, how he beat me because her
horse stumbled, how she waded through the dirt to
pluck him off me, how he swore, how she prayed that
never prayed before, how I cried, how the horses ran
away, how her bridle was burst, how I lost my crupper, with many things of worthy memory, which now
shall die in oblivion and thou return unexperienced to
thy grave.

CURTIS By this reckoning he is more shrew than she.

GRUMIO Ay, and that thou and the proudest of you all
shall find when he comes home. But what talk I of 78
this? Call forth Nathaniel, Joseph, Nicholas, Philip,
Walter, Sugarsop, and the rest. Let their heads be
sleekly combed, their blue coats brushed, and their 81
garters of an indifferent knit; let them curtsy with their 82
left legs, and not presume to touch a hair of my master's horsetail till they kiss their hands. Are they all
ready?

CURTIS They are.

GRUMIO Call them forth.

CURTIS Do you hear, ho? You must meet my master to
countenance my mistress.   89

GRUMIO Why, she hath a face of her own.

CURTIS Who knows not that?

GRUMIO Thou, it seems, that calls for company to countenance her.

CURTIS I call them forth to credit her.   94

Enter four or five Servingmen.

GRUMIO Why, she comes to borrow nothing of them.

NATHANIEL Welcome home, Grumio!

---

64 crossed thwarted, interrupted **67 bemoiled** befouled with mire
78 what why **81 blue coats** (Usual dress for servingmen.) **82 indifferent** i.e., well matched and not flamboyant **89 countenance** pay
respects to (with a following pun on the meaning "face") **94 credit**
pay respects to (with another pun following, on "extending financial
credit")

PHILIP   How now, Grumio!

JOSEPH   What, Grumio!

NICHOLAS   Fellow Grumio!

NATHANIEL   How now, old lad?

GRUMIO   Welcome, you; how now, you; what, you; fellow, you—and thus much for greeting. Now, my spruce companions, is all ready and all things neat?   103

NATHANIEL   All things is ready. How near is our master?

GRUMIO   E'en at hand, alighted by this; and therefore be not—Cock's passion, silence! I hear my master.   107

Enter Petruchio and Kate.

PETRUCHIO
   Where be these knaves? What, no man at door
   To hold my stirrup, nor to take my horse?   109
   Where is Nathaniel, Gregory, Philip?

ALL SERVANTS   Here, here, sir; here, sir.

PETRUCHIO
   Here, sir! Here, sir! Here, sir! Here, sir!
   You loggerheaded and unpolished grooms!
   What, no attendance? No regard? No duty?
   Where is the foolish knave I sent before?   115

GRUMIO
   Here, sir, as foolish as I was before.

PETRUCHIO
   You peasant swain, you whoreson malt-horse drudge!   117
   Did I not bid thee meet me in the park
   And bring along these rascal knaves with thee?

GRUMIO
   Nathaniel's coat, sir, was not fully made,
   And Gabriel's pumps were all unpinked i' the heel.   121
   There was no link to color Peter's hat,   122
   And Walter's dagger was not come from sheathing.   123

---

103 spruce lively   **107 Cock's passion** by God's (Christ's) suffering
109 hold my stirrup i.e., help me dismount   **115 before** ahead (with pun in next line on "previously")   **117 swain** rustic.   **whoreson . . . drudge** worthless plodding work animal, such as would be used on a treadmill to grind malt   **121 pumps** lowcut shoes.   **unpinked** lacking in eyelets or in ornamental tracing in the leather   **122 link** torch, the smoke or soot of which was used as blackening   **123 sheathing** being fitted with a sheath

There were none fine but Adam, Ralph, and Gregory;   124
The rest were ragged, old, and beggarly.
Yet, as they are, here are they come to meet you.

PETRUCHIO
Go, rascals, go, and fetch my supper in.

Exeunt Servants.

[*Sings.*] "Where is the life that late I led?
Where are those—" Sit down, Kate, and welcome.—

[*They sit at table.*]

Soud, soud, soud, soud!   130

Enter Servants with supper.

Why, when, I say?—Nay, good sweet Kate, be merry.—
Off with my boots, you rogues! You villains, when?

[*A Servant takes off Petruchio's boots.*]

[*Sings.*] "It was the friar of orders gray,   133
    As he forth walkèd on his way—"   134
Out, you rogue! You pluck my foot awry.   135

[*He kicks the Servant.*]

Take that, and mend the plucking off the other.
Be merry, Kate.—Some water, here; what, ho!

Enter one with water.

Where's my spaniel Troilus? Sirrah, get you hence,
And bid my cousin Ferdinand come hither—

[*Exit Servant.*]

One, Kate, that you must kiss and be acquainted with.
Where are my slippers? Shall I have some water?
Come, Kate, and wash, and welcome heartily.

[*Servant offers water, but spills some.*]

You whoreson villain, will you let it fall?

[*He strikes the Servant.*]

KATHARINA
Patience, I pray you, 'twas a fault unwilling.   144

PETRUCHIO
A whoreson, beetle-headed, flap-eared knave!—   145

124 fine well clothed   **130 Soud** (A nonsense song, or expression of
impatience, or perhaps "food!")   **133–134 "It . . . way"** (A fragment of a
bawdy ballad.)   **135 Out** (Exclamation of anger or reproach.)   **144 unwilling** accidental   **145 beetle-headed** i.e., blockheaded (since a *beetle* is
a pounding tool)

Come, Kate, sit down. I know you have a stomach.   146
Will you give thanks, sweet Kate, or else shall I?—   147
What's this? Mutton?

FIRST SERVANT   Ay.

PETRUCHIO   Who brought it?

PETER   I.

PETRUCHIO
'Tis burnt, and so is all the meat.
What dogs are these? Where is the rascal cook?
How durst you, villains, bring it from the dresser   151
And serve it thus to me that love it not?
There, take it to you, trenchers, cups, and all.   153
        [*He throws the meat, etc., at them.*]
You heedless joltheads and unmannered slaves!   154
What, do you grumble? I'll be with you straight.   155
                [*They run out.*]

KATHARINA
I pray you, husband, be not so disquiet.
The meat was well, if you were so contented.

PETRUCHIO
I tell thee, Kate, 'twas burnt and dried away,
And I expressly am forbid to touch it;
For it engenders choler, planteth anger,   160
And better 'twere that both of us did fast,
Since, of ourselves, ourselves are choleric,
Than feed it with such overroasted flesh.
Be patient. Tomorrow 't shall be mended,
And for this night we'll fast for company.
Come, I will bring thee to thy bridal chamber.
                                Exeunt.

        Enter Servants severally.

NATHANIEL   Peter, didst ever see the like?
PETER   He kills her in her own humor.   168

146 **stomach** appetite (with a suggestion also of "temper")   147 **give
thanks** say grace   151 **dresser** sideboard   153 **trenchers** wooden dishes
or plates   154 **joltheads** blockheads   155 **with you straight** after you at
once (to get even for this)   160 **choler** the humor or bodily fluid, hot
and dry in character, that supposedly produced ill temper and was
thought to be aggravated by the eating of roast meat   168 **kills . . .
humor** i.e., uses anger to subdue anger in her

Enter Curtis.

GRUMIO   Where is he?

CURTIS   In her chamber, making a sermon of continency   170
to her,

And rails, and swears, and rates, that she, poor soul,   172
Knows not which way to stand, to look, to speak,
And sits as one new risen from a dream.
Away, away! For he is coming hither.   [*Exeunt.*]

Enter Petruchio.

PETRUCHIO
Thus have I politicly begun my reign,
And 'tis my hope to end successfully.
My falcon now is sharp and passing empty,   178
And till she stoop she must not be full-gorged,   179
For then she never looks upon her lure.
Another way I have to man my haggard,   181
To make her come and know her keeper's call:
That is, to watch her, as we watch these kites   183
That bate and beat and will not be obedient.   184
She ate no meat today, nor none shall eat.
Last night she slept not, nor tonight she shall not.
As with the meat, some undeservèd fault
I'll find about the making of the bed,
And here I'll fling the pillow, there the bolster,
This way the coverlet, another way the sheets.
Ay, and amid this hurly I intend   191
That all is done in reverent care of her.
And in conclusion she shall watch all night,
And if she chance to nod I'll rail and brawl,
And with the clamor keep her still awake.
This is a way to kill a wife with kindness;
And thus I'll curb her mad and headstrong humor.   197

---

170 sermon of continency lecture on self-restraint   **172 rates** scolds
178 sharp hungry   **179 stoop** fly down to the lure   **181 man** tame (with
a pun on the sense of "assert masculine authority").   **haggard** wild
female hawk; hence, an intractable woman   **183 watch her** keep her
watching, i.e., awake.   **kites** a kind of hawk (with a pun on *Kate*)
184 bate and beat beat the wings impatiently and flutter away from the
hand or perch   **191 intend** pretend   **197 humor** disposition

He that knows better how to tame a shrew,
Now let him speak; 'tis charity to show.   *Exit.* 199

❖

4.2   *Enter Tranio [as Lucentio] and Hortensio [as
          Litio].*

TRANIO
  Is 't possible, friend Litio, that Mistress Bianca
  Doth fancy any other but Lucentio?
  I tell you, sir, she bears me fair in hand.   3
HORTENSIO
  Sir, to satisfy you in what I have said,
  Stand by and mark the manner of his teaching.
                                        [They stand aside.]

     Enter Bianca [and Lucentio as Cambio].

LUCENTIO
  Now, mistress, profit you in what you read?   6
BIANCA
  What, master, read you? First resolve me that.   7
LUCENTIO
  I read that I profess, the Art to Love.   8
BIANCA
  And may you prove, sir, master of your art!
LUCENTIO
  While you, sweet dear, prove mistress of my heart!
                [They move aside and court each other.]
HORTENSIO *[To Tranio, coming forward]*
  Quick proceeders, marry! Now tell me, I pray,   11
  You that durst swear that your mistress Bianca
  Loved none in the world so well as Lucentio.

---

199 'tis charity to show it's benevolent to share such wisdom. (On the
rhyme with *shrew*, see also the play's final lines.)

4.2. Location: Padua. Before Baptista's house.
3 bears . . . hand gives me encouragement, leads me on   **6 read** (Evidently, both Bianca and "Cambio" carry books.)   **7 resolve** answer
8 that I profess what I practice.   **Art to Love** Ovid's *Ars Amandi*
11 proceeders (1) workers, doers (2) candidates for academic degrees (as
suggested by the phrase *master of your art* in l. 9)

TRANIO
O despiteful love! Unconstant womankind!   14
I tell thee, Litio, this is wonderful.   15

HORTENSIO
Mistake no more. I am not Litio,
Nor a musician, as I seem to be,
But one that scorn to live in this disguise   18
For such a one as leaves a gentleman   19
And makes a god of such a cullion.   20
Know, sir, that I am called Hortensio.

TRANIO
Signor Hortensio, I have often heard
Of your entire affection to Bianca;   23
And since mine eyes are witness of her lightness,   24
I will with you, if you be so contented,
Forswear Bianca and her love forever.

HORTENSIO
See how they kiss and court! Signor Lucentio,
Here is my hand, and here I firmly vow
                    [*Giving his hand*]
Never to woo her more, but do forswear her
As one unworthy all the former favors
That I have fondly flattered her withal.   31

TRANIO
And here I take the like unfeignèd oath,
Never to marry with her though she would entreat.
Fie on her, see how beastly she doth court him!

HORTENSIO
Would all the world but he had quite forsworn!   35
For me, that I may surely keep mine oath,
I will be married to a wealthy widow,
Ere three days pass, which hath as long loved me
As I have loved this proud disdainful haggard.   39
And so farewell, Signor Lucentio.
Kindness in women, not their beauteous looks,

___

14 despiteful cruel **15 wonderful** cause for wonder **18 scorn** scorns
19 such a one i.e., Bianca **20 cullion** base fellow (referring to "Cambio"; literally the word means "testicle") **23 entire** sincere **24 lightness** wantonness **31 fondly** foolishly **35 Would . . . forsworn** i.e., may everyone in the world forsake her except the penniless "Cambio," and may she thus get what she deserves **39 haggard** wild hawk

Shall win my love. And so I take my leave,
In resolution as I swore before.   [*Exit.*] 43

TRANIO   [*As Lucentio and Bianca come forward again*]
Mistress Bianca, bless you with such grace
As 'longeth to a lover's blessèd case! 45
Nay, I have ta'en you napping, gentle love, 46
And have forsworn you with Hortensio.

BIANCA
Tranio, you jest. But have you both forsworn me?

TRANIO
Mistress, we have.

LUCENTIO   Then we are rid of Litio.

TRANIO
I' faith, he'll have a lusty widow now, 50
That shall be wooed and wedded in a day.

BIANCA   God give him joy!

TRANIO   Ay, and he'll tame her.

BIANCA   He says so, Tranio?

TRANIO
Faith, he is gone unto the taming school.

BIANCA
The taming school! What, is there such a place?

TRANIO
Ay, mistress, and Petruchio is the master,
That teacheth tricks eleven-and-twenty long, 58
To tame a shrew and charm her chattering tongue.

    Enter Biondello.

BIONDELLO
O master, master, I have watched so long
That I am dog-weary, but at last I spied
An ancient angel coming down the hill 62
Will serve the turn.

TRANIO   What is he, Biondello? 63

---

43 In resolution determined   **45 'longeth** belongs   **46 ta'en you napping** i.e., surprised you   **50 lusty** merry, lively   **58 eleven . . . long** i.e., in sufficient number (alluding to the card game called "one-and-thirty" referred to at 1.2.32–33)   **62 ancient angel** i.e., fellow of the good old stamp. (Literally, an "angel" or gold coin bearing the stamp of the archangel Michael and thus distinguishable from more recent debased coinage.)   **63 Will . . . turn** who will serve our purposes

BIONDELLO
  Master, a marcantant, or a pedant,   64
  I know not what, but formal in apparel,
  In gait and countenance surely like a father.
LUCENTIO And what of him, Tranio?
TRANIO
  If he be credulous and trust my tale,
  I'll make him glad to seem Vincentio
  And give assurance to Baptista Minola
  As if he were the right Vincentio.
  Take in your love, and then let me alone.   72

               [Exeunt Lucentio and Bianca.]

    Enter a Pedant.

PEDANT
  God save you, sir!
TRANIO   And you sir! You are welcome.
  Travel you far on, or are you at the farthest?
PEDANT
  Sir, at the farthest for a week or two,
  But then up farther, and as far as Rome,
  And so to Tripoli, if God lend me life.
TRANIO
  What countryman, I pray?
PEDANT   Of Mantua.
TRANIO
  Of Mantua, sir? Marry, God forbid!
  And come to Padua, careless of your life?
PEDANT
  My life, sir! How, I pray? For that goes hard.   81
TRANIO
  'Tis death for anyone in Mantua
  To come to Padua. Know you not the cause?
  Your ships are stayed at Venice, and the Duke,   84
  For private quarrel twixt your duke and him,
  Hath published and proclaimed it openly.
  'Tis marvel, but that you are but newly come,
  You might have heard it else proclaimed about.

---

64 marcantant merchant. **pedant** schoolmaster (though at ll. 90–91 he
speaks more like a merchant) **72 let me alone** i.e., count on me
81 goes hard is serious indeed **84 stayed** detained

PEDANT
Alas, sir, it is worse for me than so,
For I have bills for money by exchange   90
From Florence, and must here deliver them.

TRANIO
Well, sir, to do you courtesy,
This will I do, and this I will advise you—
First, tell me, have you ever been at Pisa?

PEDANT
Ay, sir, in Pisa have I often been,
Pisa renownèd for grave citizens.

TRANIO
Among them know you one Vincentio?

PEDANT
I know him not, but I have heard of him;
A merchant of incomparable wealth.

TRANIO
He is my father, sir, and, sooth to say,
In count'nance somewhat doth resemble you.

BIONDELLO [*Aside*]   As much as an apple doth an oyster,
and all one.   103

TRANIO
To save your life in this extremity,
This favor will I do you for his sake;
And think it not the worst of all your fortunes
That you are like to Sir Vincentio.
His name and credit shall you undertake,   108
And in my house you shall be friendly lodged.
Look that you take upon you as you should.   110
You understand me, sir. So shall you stay
Till you have done your business in the city.
If this be courtesy, sir, accept of it.

PEDANT
O sir, I do, and will repute you ever
The patron of my life and liberty.

TRANIO
Then go with me to make the matter good.   116
This, by the way, I let you understand:

90 bills . . . exchange promissory notes **103 all one** no matter
108 credit reputation **110 take upon you** play your part **116 make . . .
good** carry out the plan

My father is here looked for every day,
To pass assurance of a dower in marriage   119
Twixt me and one Baptista's daughter here.
In all these circumstances I'll instruct you.
Go with me to clothe you as becomes you.

                                        Exeunt.

❖

4.3   *Enter Katharina and Grumio.*

GRUMIO
  No, no, forsooth, I dare not for my life.
KATHARINA
  The more my wrong, the more his spite appears.   2
  What, did he marry me to famish me?
  Beggars that come unto my father's door
  Upon entreaty have a present alms;   5
  If not, elsewhere they meet with charity.
  But I, who never knew how to entreat,
  Nor never needed that I should entreat,
  Am starved for meat, giddy for lack of sleep,   9
  With oaths kept waking, and with brawling fed.
  And that which spites me more than all these wants,
  He does it under name of perfect love,
  As who should say, if I should sleep or eat,   13
  'Twere deadly sickness or else present death.
  I prithee, go and get me some repast,
  I care not what, so it be wholesome food.
GRUMIO   What say you to a neat's foot?   17
KATHARINA
  'Tis passing good; I prithee, let me have it.
GRUMIO
  I fear it is too choleric a meat.
  How say you to a fat tripe finely broiled?
KATHARINA
  I like it well, good Grumio, fetch it me.

---

119 pass assurance convey a legal guarantee

4.3. Location: Petruchio's house. A table is set out, with seats.
2 my wrong the wrong done to me   **5 present** immediate (as in l. 14)
9 meat food   **13 As who** as if one   **17 neat's** ox's

GRUMIO
I cannot tell. I fear 'tis choleric.
What say you to a piece of beef and mustard?

KATHARINA
A dish that I do love to feed upon.

GRUMIO
Ay, but the mustard is too hot a little.

KATHARINA
Why then, the beef, and let the mustard rest.

GRUMIO
Nay then, I will not; you shall have the mustard
Or else you get no beef of Grumio.

KATHARINA
Then both, or one, or anything thou wilt.

GRUMIO
Why then, the mustard without the beef.

KATHARINA
Go, get thee gone, thou false deluding slave,

Beats him.

That feed'st me with the very name of meat!
Sorrow on thee and all the pack of you,
That triumph thus upon my misery!
Go, get thee gone, I say.

Enter Petruchio and Hortensio with meat.

PETRUCHIO
How fares my Kate? What, sweeting, all amort?   36

HORTENSIO
Mistress, what cheer?   Faith, as cold as can be.

KATHARINA

PETRUCHIO
Pluck up thy spirits; look cheerfully upon me.
Here, love, thou see'st how diligent I am
To dress thy meat myself and bring it thee.   40
I am sure, sweet Kate, this kindness merits thanks.
What, not a word? Nay, then thou lov'st it not,
And all my pains is sorted to no proof.   43
Here, take away this dish.

KATHARINA   I pray you, let it stand.

36 all amort dejected, dispirited **40 dress** prepare **43 sorted to no
proof** proved to be to no purpose

PETRUCHIO
  The poorest service is repaid with thanks,
  And so shall mine before you touch the meat.
KATHARINA I thank you, sir.
HORTENSIO
  Signor Petruchio, fie, you are to blame.
  Come, Mistress Kate, I'll bear you company.
                                 [*They sit at table.*]
PETRUCHIO [*Aside to Hortensio*]
  Eat it up all, Hortensio, if thou lovest me.—
  Much good do it unto thy gentle heart!
  Kate, eat apace. And now, my honey love,
  Will we return unto thy father's house
  And revel it as bravely as the best,   54
  With silken coats and caps and golden rings,
  With ruffs and cuffs and farthingales and things,   56
  With scarves and fans and double change of bravery,   57
  With amber bracelets, beads, and all this knavery.
  What, hast thou dined? The tailor stays thy leisure,
  To deck thy body with his ruffling treasure.   60

     Enter Tailor [*with a gown*].

  Come, tailor, let us see these ornaments.
  Lay forth the gown.

     Enter Haberdasher [*with a cap*].

               What news with you, sir?
HABERDASHER
  Here is the cap your worship did bespeak.
PETRUCHIO
  Why, this was molded on a porringer—   64
  A velvet dish. Fie, fie, 'tis lewd and filthy.   65
  Why, 'tis a cockle or a walnut shell,   66
  A knack, a toy, a trick, a baby's cap.   67
  Away with it! Come, let me have a bigger.
KATHARINA
  I'll have no bigger. This doth fit the time,   69
  And gentlewomen wear such caps as these.

---

54 **bravely** splendidly dressed 56 **farthingales** hooped petticoats
57 **bravery** finery 60 **ruffling treasure** finery trimmed with ruffles
64 **porringer** porridge bowl 65 **lewd** vile 66 **cockle** cockleshell
67 **trick** trifle 69 **fit the time** suit the current fashion

PETRUCHIO
  When you are gentle; you shall have one too,
  And not till then.
HORTENSIO [*Aside*] That will not be in haste.
KATHARINA
  Why, sir, I trust I may have leave to speak,
  And speak I will. I am no child, no babe.
  Your betters have endured me say my mind,
  And if you cannot, best you stop your ears.
  My tongue will tell the anger of my heart,
  Or else my heart, concealing it, will break,
  And rather than it shall, I will be free
  Even to the uttermost, as I please, in words.
PETRUCHIO
  Why, thou sayst true. It is a paltry cap,
  A custard-coffin, a bauble, a silken pie.   82
  I love thee well in that thou lik'st it not.
KATHARINA
  Love me or love me not, I like the cap,
  And it I will have, or I will have none.
                                        [*Exit Haberdasher.*]
PETRUCHIO
  Thy gown? Why, ay. Come, tailor, let us see 't.
  O, mercy, God, what masquing stuff is here?   87
  What's this, a sleeve? 'Tis like a demi-cannon.   88
  What, up and down carved like an apple tart?   89
  Here's snip and nip and cut and slish and slash,
  Like to a censer in a barber's shop.   91
  Why, what i' devil's name, tailor, call'st thou this?   92
HORTENSIO [*Aside*]
  I see she's like to have neither cap nor gown.
TAILOR
  You bid me make it orderly and well,
  According to the fashion and the time.
PETRUCHIO
  Marry, and did. But if you be remembered,   96

---

82 custard-coffin pastry crust for a custard **87 masquing** i.e., suited
only for a masque **88 demi-cannon** large cannon **89 up and down** all
over, exactly. **like an apple tart** i.e., with slashing or slits like the slits
on the crust of fruit tarts, here revealing the brighter fabric under-
neath **91 censer** perfuming pan having an ornamental lid **92 i'** in
(the) **96 be remembered** recollect

I did not bid you mar it to the time.
Go, hop me over every kennel home,   98
For you shall hop without my custom, sir.
I'll none of it. Hence, make your best of it.

KATHARINA
I never saw a better-fashioned gown,
More quaint, more pleasing, nor more commendable.   102
Belike you mean to make a puppet of me.

PETRUCHIO
Why, true, he means to make a puppet of thee.

TAILOR
She says your worship means to make a puppet of her.

PETRUCHIO
O, monstrous arrogance! Thou liest, thou thread, thou
    thimble,
Thou yard, three-quarters, half-yard, quarter, nail!   107
Thou flea, thou nit, thou winter cricket thou!   108
Braved in mine own house with a skein of thread?   109
Away, thou rag, thou quantity, thou remnant,   110
Or I shall so be-mete thee with thy yard   111
As thou shalt think on prating whilst thou liv'st!   112
I tell thee, I, that thou hast marred her gown.

TAILOR
Your worship is deceived. The gown is made
Just as my master had direction.
Grumio gave order how it should be done.

GRUMIO   I gave him no order. I gave him the stuff.

TAILOR
But how did you desire it should be made?

GRUMIO   Marry, sir, with needle and thread.

TAILOR
But did you not request to have it cut?

GRUMIO   Thou hast faced many things.   121

TAILOR   I have.

GRUMIO   Face not me. Thou hast braved many men;   123

---

98 hop . . . home hop on home over every street gutter   102 quaint
elegant   107 nail a measure of length for cloth: 2¼ inches   108 nit
louse egg   109 Braved defied.   with by   110 quantity fragment
111 be-mete measure, i.e., thrash.   yard yardstick   112 think on prating
i.e., remember this thrashing and think twice before talking so again
121 faced trimmed. (But Grumio puns on the meaning "bullied.")
123 Face bully.   braved dressed finely

brave not me. I will neither be faced nor braved. I say 124
unto thee, I bid thy master cut out the gown, but I did
not bid him cut it to pieces. Ergo, thou liest. 126

TAILOR Why, here is the note of the fashion to testify.
[*He displays his bill.*]

PETRUCHIO Read it.

GRUMIO The note lies in 's throat if he say I said so.

TAILOR [*Reads*] "Imprimis, a loose-bodied gown—"

GRUMIO Master, if ever I said loose-bodied gown, 131
sew me in the skirts of it and beat me to death with
a bottom of brown thread. I said a gown. 133

PETRUCHIO Proceed.

TAILOR [*Reads*] "With a small compassed cape—" 135

GRUMIO I confess the cape.

TAILOR [*Reads*] "With a trunk sleeve—" 137

GRUMIO I confess two sleeves.

TAILOR [*Reads*] "The sleeves curiously cut." 139

PETRUCHIO Ay, there's the villainy.

GRUMIO Error i' the bill, sir, error i' the bill. I commanded the sleeves should be cut out and sewed up
again, and that I'll prove upon thee, though thy little 143
finger be armed in a thimble.

TAILOR This is true that I say. An I had thee in place 145
where, thou shouldst know it. 146

GRUMIO I am for thee straight. Take thou the bill, give 147
me thy mete-yard, and spare not me. 148

HORTENSIO God-a-mercy, Grumio, then he shall have
no odds.

PETRUCHIO Well, sir, in brief, the gown is not for me.

GRUMIO You are i' the right, sir, 'tis for my mistress.

PETRUCHIO Go, take it up unto thy master's use. 153

GRUMIO Villain, not for thy life! Take up my mistress'
gown for thy master's use!

PETRUCHIO Why, sir, what's your conceit in that? 156

124 brave defy **126 Ergo** therefore **131 loose-bodied gown** (Grumio
plays on *loose*, wanton; a gown fit for a prostitute.) **133 bottom** ball
wound from a skein. (A weaver's term.) **135 compassed** with the edges
forming a semicircle **137 trunk** full, wide **139 curiously** elaborately
143 prove upon thee prove by fighting you **145–146 in place where** in a
suitable place **147 bill** (1) the note ordering the gown (2) a weapon, a
halberd **148 mete-yard** measuring stick **153 use** i.e., whatever use he
can make of it. (But Grumio deliberately misinterprets in a bawdy
sense.) **156 conceit** idea

GRUMIO
  O, sir, the conceit is deeper than you think for:
  Take up my mistress' gown to his master's use!
  O, fie, fie, fie!

PETRUCHIO [*Aside to Hortensio*]
  Hortensio, say thou wilt see the tailor paid.—
  [*To Tailor.*] Go take it hence, begone, and say no more.

HORTENSIO [*Aside to Tailor*]
  Tailor, I'll pay thee for thy gown tomorrow.
  Take no unkindness of his hasty words.
  Away, I say. Commend me to thy master.

                        Exit Tailor.

PETRUCHIO
  Well, come, my Kate. We will unto your father's
  Even in these honest mean habiliments.   166
  Our purses shall be proud, our garments poor,
  For 'tis the mind that makes the body rich;
  And as the sun breaks through the darkest clouds,
  So honor peereth in the meanest habit.   170
  What, is the jay more precious than the lark
  Because his feathers are more beautiful?
  Or is the adder better than the eel
  Because his painted skin contents the eye?   174
  O, no, good Kate; neither art thou the worse
  For this poor furniture and mean array.   176
  If thou account'st it shame, lay it on me.
  And therefore frolic; we will hence forthwith,
  To feast and sport us at thy father's house.
  [*To Grumio.*] Go call my men, and let us straight to him;
  And bring our horses unto Long Lane end.
  There will we mount, and thither walk on foot.
  Let's see, I think 'tis now some seven o'clock,
  And well we may come there by dinnertime.   184

KATHARINA
  I dare assure you, sir, 'tis almost two,
  And 'twill be suppertime ere you come there.

PETRUCHIO
  It shall be seven ere I go to horse.

166 honest mean habiliments respectable, plain clothes   **170 peereth** is
seen.   **habit** attire   **174 painted** patterned   **176 furniture** furnishings
of attire   **184 dinnertime** i.e., about noon

Look what I speak, or do, or think to do,   188
You are still crossing it.—Sirs, let 't alone.   189
I will not go today, and ere I do
It shall be what o'clock I say it is.

HORTENSIO [Aside]
Why, so this gallant will command the sun.

                          [Exeunt.]

❖

4.4   *Enter Tranio [as Lucentio], and the Pedant*
         dressed like Vincentio [booted].

TRANIO
Sir, this is the house. Please it you that I call?

PEDANT
Ay, what else? And but I be deceived,   2
Signor Baptista may remember me,   3
Near twenty years ago, in Genoa,
Where we were lodgers at the Pegasus.   5

TRANIO
'Tis well; and hold your own in any case   6
With such austerity as 'longeth to a father.

     Enter Biondello.

PEDANT
I warrant you. But, sir, here comes your boy;
'Twere good he were schooled.   9

TRANIO
Fear you not him.—Sirrah Biondello,
Now do your duty throughly, I advise you.   11
Imagine 'twere the right Vincentio.

BIONDELLO   Tut, fear not me.

---

188 Look what whatever   **189 still crossing** always contradicting or
defying

4.4. Location: Padua. Before Baptista's house.
s.d. booted (signifying travel)   **2 but** unless   **3 may remember** (The
Pedant is rehearsing what he is to say.)   **5 the Pegasus** i.e., an inn, so
named after the famous winged horse of classical myth   **6 hold your
own** play your part   **9 schooled** i.e., rehearsed in his part   **11 throughly**
thoroughly

TRANIO
But hast thou done thy errand to Baptista?

BIONDELLO
I told him that your father was at Venice,
And that you looked for him this day in Padua.

TRANIO
Thou'rt a tall fellow. Hold thee that to drink.   17
                         [*He gives money.*]
Here comes Baptista. Set your countenance, sir.

    Enter Baptista and Lucentio [as Cambio]. [The]
    Pedant [stands] bareheaded.

Signor Baptista, you are happily met.
[*To the Pedant.*] Sir, this is the gentleman I told you of.
I pray you, stand good father to me now;
Give me Bianca for my patrimony.

PEDANT   Soft, son!
Sir, by your leave, having come to Padua
To gather in some debts, my son Lucentio
Made me acquainted with a weighty cause
Of love between your daughter and himself;
And, for the good report I hear of you
And for the love he beareth to your daughter
And she to him, to stay him not too long,
I am content, in a good father's care,
To have him matched. And if you please to like
No worse than I, upon some agreement
Me shall you find ready and willing
With one consent to have her so bestowed;
For curious I cannot be with you,   36
Signor Baptista, of whom I hear so well.

BAPTISTA
Sir, pardon me in what I have to say;
Your plainness and your shortness please me well.
Right true it is your son Lucentio here
Doth love my daughter, and she loveth him,
Or both dissemble deeply their affections.
And therefore, if you say no more than this,
That like a father you will deal with him

---

17 tall fine. **Hold . . . drink** take that and buy a drink **36 curious**
overly particular

And pass my daughter a sufficient dower,   45
The match is made and all is done.
Your son shall have my daughter with consent.

TRANIO

I thank you, sir. Where then do you know best
We be affied and such assurance ta'en   49
As shall with either part's agreement stand?

BAPTISTA

Not in my house, Lucentio, for you know
Pitchers have ears, and I have many servants.
Besides, old Gremio is hearkening still,   53
And happily we might be interrupted.   54

TRANIO

Then at my lodging, an it like you.   55
There doth my father lie, and there this night   56
We'll pass the business privately and well.   57
Send for your daughter by your servant here.
         [*He indicates Lucentio, and winks at him.*]
My boy shall fetch the scrivener presently.   59
The worst is this, that at so slender warning
You are like to have a thin and slender pittance.   61

BAPTISTA

It likes me well. Cambio, hie you home,
And bid Bianca make her ready straight.
And if you will, tell what hath happened:
Lucentio's father is arrived in Padua,
And how she's like to be Lucentio's wife.
                          [*Exit Lucentio.*]

BIONDELLO

I pray the gods she may, with all my heart!

TRANIO

Dally not with the gods, but get thee gone.
                         Exit [*Biondello*].
Signor Baptista, shall I lead the way?
Welcome! One mess is like to be your cheer.   70
Come, sir, we will better it in Pisa.

---

45 pass settle on, give   **49 affied** betrothed   **53 hearkening still** continually listening   **54 happily** haply, perhaps   **55 an it like** if it please
56 lie lodge   **57 pass** transact   **59 scrivener** notary, one to draw up contracts   **61 like** likely.   **slender pittance** i.e., scanty banquet
70 mess dish.   **cheer** entertainment

BAPTISTA I follow you.
                    Exeunt [Tranio, Pedant, and Baptista].

          Enter Lucentio [as Cambio] and Biondello.

BIONDELLO Cambio!
LUCENTIO What sayst thou, Biondello?
BIONDELLO You saw my master wink and laugh upon
     you?
LUCENTIO Biondello, what of that?
BIONDELLO Faith, nothing; but he's left me here behind
     to expound the meaning or moral of his signs and   79
     tokens.
LUCENTIO I pray thee, moralize them.   81
BIONDELLO Then thus. Baptista is safe, talking with the   82
     deceiving father of a deceitful son.
LUCENTIO And what of him?
BIONDELLO His daughter is to be brought by you to the
     supper.
LUCENTIO And then?
BIONDELLO The old priest at Saint Luke's church is at
     your command at all hours.
LUCENTIO And what of all this?
BIONDELLO I cannot tell, except they are busied about a   91
     counterfeit assurance. Take you assurance of her,   92
     cum privilegio ad imprimendum solum. To the   93
     church take the priest, clerk, and some sufficient hon- 94
     est witnesses.
     If this be not that you look for, I have no more to say,
     But bid Bianca farewell forever and a day.
                              [Biondello starts to leave.]
LUCENTIO Hear'st thou, Biondello?
BIONDELLO I cannot tarry. I knew a wench married in
     an afternoon as she went to the garden for parsley to
     stuff a rabbit, and so may you, sir. And so, adieu, sir.
     My master hath appointed me to go to Saint Luke's, to

79 moral hidden meaning   **81 moralize** elucidate   **82 safe** i.e., safely
deceived   **91 except** unless   **92 counterfeit assurance** pretended be-
trothal agreement.   **Take . . . of her** legalize your claim to her (by
marriage)   **93 cum . . . solum** with exclusive printing rights. (A copy-
right formula often appearing on the title pages of books, here jokingly
applied to the marriage.)   **94 sufficient** financially competent, well-to-do

bid the priest be ready to come against you come with 103
your appendix.   *Exit.* 104

LUCENTIO
I may, and will, if she be so contented.
She will be pleased; then wherefore should I doubt?
Hap what hap may, I'll roundly go about her.   107
It shall go hard if Cambio go without her.   *Exit.* 108

❖

4.5   *Enter Petruchio, Kate, and Hortensio.*

PETRUCHIO
Come on, i' God's name, once more toward our father's.   1
Good Lord, how bright and goodly shines the moon!

KATHARINA
The moon? The sun. It is not moonlight now.

PETRUCHIO
I say it is the moon that shines so bright.

KATHARINA
I know it is the sun that shines so bright.

PETRUCHIO
Now, by my mother's son, and that's myself,
It shall be moon, or star, or what I list,   7
Or ere I journey to your father's house.—   8
Go on, and fetch our horses back again—
Evermore crossed and crossed, nothing but crossed!

HORTENSIO [*To Katharina*]
Say as he says, or we shall never go.

KATHARINA
Forward, I pray, since we have come so far,
And be it moon, or sun, or what you please;
An if you please to call it a rush candle,   14
Henceforth I vow it shall be so for me.

---

103 against you come in anticipation of your arrival   **104 appendix**
something appended, i.e., the bride (continuing the metaphor of printing)   **107 roundly . . . her** set about marrying her in no uncertain
terms   **108 go hard** be unfortunate (with bawdy pun)

4.5. Location: A road on the way to Padua.
1 our father's our father's house   **7 list** please   **8 Or ere** before
14 rush candle a rush dipped into tallow; hence a very feeble light

PETRUCHIO
  I say it is the moon.

KATHARINA   I know it is the moon.

PETRUCHIO
  Nay, then you lie. It is the blessèd sun.

KATHARINA
  Then, God be blest, it is the blessèd sun.
  But sun it is not when you say it is not,
  And the moon changes even as your mind.
  What you will have it named, even that it is,
  And so it shall be so for Katharine.

HORTENSIO
  Petruchio, go thy ways, the field is won.

PETRUCHIO
  Well, forward, forward, thus the bowl should run,
  And not unluckily against the bias.   25
  But, soft! Company is coming here.

    Enter Vincentio.

  [*To Vincentio.*] Good morrow, gentle mistress. Where
      away?—   27
  Tell me, sweet Kate, and tell me truly too,
  Hast thou beheld a fresher gentlewoman?
  Such war of white and red within her cheeks!
  What stars do spangle heaven with such beauty
  As those two eyes become that heavenly face?—
  Fair lovely maid, once more good day to thee.—
  Sweet Kate, embrace her for her beauty's sake.

HORTENSIO [*Aside*]
  'A will make the man mad, to make a woman of him.   35

KATHARINA [*Embracing Vincentio*]
  Young budding virgin, fair and fresh and sweet,
  Whither away, or where is thy abode?
  Happy the parents of so fair a child!
  Happier the man whom favorable stars
  Allots thee for his lovely bedfellow!

---

25 against the bias off its proper course. (The *bias* is an off-center
weight in a bowling ball enabling the bowler to roll the ball in an
oblique or curving path; it runs *unluckily*, that is, unsuccessfully,
against the bias when it encounters an obstacle.)   **27 Where away**
where are you going   **35 'A** he

PETRUCHIO
  Why, how now, Kate? I hope thou art not mad.
  This is a man, old, wrinkled, faded, withered,
  And not a maiden, as thou sayst he is.

KATHARINA
  Pardon, old father, my mistaking eyes,
  That have been so bedazzled with the sun
  That everything I look on seemeth green.   46
  Now I perceive thou art a reverend father.
  Pardon, I pray thee, for my mad mistaking.

PETRUCHIO
  Do, good old grandsire, and withal make known
  Which way thou travelest—if along with us,
  We shall be joyful of thy company.

VINCENTIO
  Fair sir, and you my merry mistress,
  That with your strange encounter much amazed me,
  My name is called Vincentio; my dwelling Pisa,
  And bound I am to Padua, there to visit
  A son of mine, which long I have not seen.

PETRUCHIO
  What is his name?

VINCENTIO   Lucentio, gentle sir.

PETRUCHIO
  Happily met, the happier for thy son.
  And now by law, as well as reverend age,
  I may entitle thee my loving father.
  The sister to my wife, this gentlewoman,
  Thy son by this hath married. Wonder not,   62
  Nor be not grieved. She is of good esteem,   63
  Her dowry wealthy, and of worthy birth;
  Besides, so qualified as may beseem   65
  The spouse of any noble gentleman.
  Let me embrace with old Vincentio,
  And wander we to see thy honest son,
  Who will of thy arrival be full joyous.
                          [*He embraces Vincentio.*]

VINCENTIO
  But is this true? Or is it else your pleasure,

---

46 green young and fresh   **62 by this** by this time   **63 esteem** reputation   **65 beseem** befit

Like pleasant travelers, to break a jest
Upon the company you overtake?

HORTENSIO
I do assure thee, father, so it is.

PETRUCHIO
Come, go along, and see the truth hereof,
For our first merriment hath made thee jealous.   75

Exeunt [all but Hortensio].

HORTENSIO
Well, Petruchio, this has put me in heart.
Have to my widow! And if she be froward,   77
Then hast thou taught Hortensio to be untoward.   78

Exit.

✤

---

75 jealous suspicious   **77 Have to** i.e., now for.   **froward** perverse
78 untoward unmannerly

5.1 *Enter Biondello, Lucentio [no longer
disguised], and Bianca. Gremio is out before
[and stands aside].*

BIONDELLO Softly and swiftly, sir, for the priest is
ready.

LUCENTIO I fly, Biondello. But they may chance to need
thee at home; therefore leave us.

BIONDELLO Nay, faith, I'll see the church a' your back, 5
and then come back to my master's as soon as I can.
                [Exeunt Lucentio, Bianca, and Biondello.]

GREMIO
I marvel Cambio comes not all this while.

    *Enter Petruchio, Kate, Vincentio, Grumio, with
    attendants.*

PETRUCHIO
Sir, here's the door; this is Lucentio's house.
My father's bears more toward the marketplace; 9
Thither must I, and here I leave you, sir.

VINCENTIO
You shall not choose but drink before you go.
I think I shall command your welcome here,
And, by all likelihood, some cheer is toward. 13
                              Knock.

GREMIO *[Advancing]* They're busy within. You were
best knock louder. 15

    Pedant looks out of the window.

PEDANT What's he that knocks as he would beat down
the gate?

VINCENTIO Is Signor Lucentio within, sir?

PEDANT He's within, sir, but not to be spoken withal.

5.1. Location: Padua. Before Lucentio's house.
s.d. out before i.e., onstage first. (Gremio does not see Biondello, Lucentio, and Bianca as they steal to church, or else does not recognize Lucentio in his own person.) **5 a' your back** at your back, behind you (i.e., I'll see you in church and safely married) **9 father's** i.e., father-in-law's, Baptista's. **bears** lies. (A nautical term.) **13 toward** in prospect **15 s.d. window** i.e., probably the gallery to the rear, over the stage

VINCENTIO What if a man bring him a hundred pound
or two, to make merry withal?

PEDANT Keep your hundred pounds to yourself. He
shall need none, so long as I live.

PETRUCHIO [*To Vincentio*] Nay, I told you your son was
well beloved in Padua.—Do you hear, sir? To leave
frivolous circumstances, I pray you, tell Signor 26
Lucentio that his father is come from Pisa and is here
at the door to speak with him.

PEDANT Thou liest. His father is come from Padua and
here looking out at the window.

VINCENTIO Art thou his father?

PEDANT Ay, sir, so his mother says, if I may believe
her.

PETRUCHIO [*To Vincentio*] Why, how now, gentleman!
Why, this is flat knavery, to take upon you another 35
man's name.

PEDANT Lay hands on the villain. I believe 'a means to
cozen somebody in this city under my countenance. 38

Enter Biondello.

BIONDELLO [*To himself*] I have seen them in the church
together, God send 'em good shipping! But who is 40
here? Mine old master Vincentio! Now we are undone
and brought to nothing.

VINCENTIO [*Seeing Biondello*] Come hither, crack-hemp. 43

BIONDELLO I hope I may choose, sir. 44

VINCENTIO Come hither, you rogue. What, have you
forgot me?

BIONDELLO Forgot you? No, sir. I could not forget you,
for I never saw you before in all my life.

VINCENTIO What, you notorious villain, didst thou
never see thy master's father, Vincentio?

BIONDELLO What, my old worshipful old master? Yes,
marry, sir, see where he looks out of the window.

VINCENTIO Is 't so, indeed?   *He beats Biondello.*

---

26 circumstances matters **35 flat** downright **38 cozen** cheat. **under
my countenance** by pretending to be me **40 good shipping** bon voyage,
good fortune **43 crack-hemp** i.e., rogue likely to end up being hanged
44 choose do as I choose

BIONDELLO Help, help, help! Here's a madman will
    murder me.   [*Exit.*]
PEDANT Help, son! Help, Signor Baptista!
                                  [*Exit from the window.*]
PETRUCHIO Prithee, Kate, let's stand aside and see the
    end of this controversy.   [*They stand aside.*]

    Enter [below] Pedant with servants, Baptista,
    [*and*] *Tranio* [*as Lucentio*].

TRANIO Sir, what are you that offer to beat my servant? 59
VINCENTIO What am I, sir? Nay, what are you, sir? O
    immortal gods! O fine villain! A silken doublet, a vel-
    vet hose, a scarlet cloak, and a copatain hat! O, I am 62
    undone, I am undone! While I play the good husband 63
    at home, my son and my servant spend all at the uni-
    versity.
TRANIO How now, what's the matter?
BAPTISTA What, is the man lunatic?
TRANIO Sir, you seem a sober ancient gentleman by
    your habit, but your words show you a madman. 69
    Why, sir, what 'cerns it you if I wear pearl and gold? 70
    I thank my good father, I am able to maintain it. 71
VINCENTIO Thy father! O villain, he is a sailmaker in
    Bergamo.
BAPTISTA You mistake, sir, you mistake, sir. Pray, what
    do you think is his name?
VINCENTIO His name! As if I knew not his name! I have
    brought him up ever since he was three years old, and
    his name is Tranio.
PEDANT Away, away, mad ass! His name is Lucentio,
    and he is mine only son, and heir to the lands of me,
    Signor Vincentio.
VINCENTIO Lucentio! O, he hath murdered his master!
    Lay hold on him, I charge you, in the Duke's name.
    O, my son, my son! Tell me, thou villain, where is my
    son Lucentio?
TRANIO Call forth an officer.

---

59 offer dare, presume   **62 copatain** high-crowned, sugar-loaf shape
63 good husband careful provider, manager   **69 habit** clothing
70 'cerns concerns   **71 maintain** afford

[*Enter an Officer.*]

Carry this mad knave to the jail. Father Baptista, I
charge you see that he be forthcoming.   88
VINCENTIO   Carry me to the jail?
GREMIO   Stay, officer, he shall not go to prison.
BAPTISTA   Talk not, Signor Gremio, I say he shall go to
prison.
GREMIO   Take heed, Signor Baptista, lest you be coney-   93
catched in this business. I dare swear this is the right   94
Vincentio.
PEDANT   Swear, if thou dar'st.
GREMIO   Nay, I dare not swear it.
TRANIO   Then thou wert best say that I am not Lucentio.   98
GREMIO   Yes, I know thee to be Signor Lucentio.
BAPTISTA   Away with the dotard! To the jail with him!

   Enter Biondello, Lucentio, and Bianca.

VINCENTIO   Thus strangers may be haled and abused.   101
  —O monstrous villain!
BIONDELLO   O! We are spoiled and—yonder he is. Deny   103
him, forswear him, or else we are all undone.
      Exeunt Biondello, Tranio, and Pedant, as fast
         as may be. [*Lucentio and Bianca*] *kneel.*
LUCENTIO
Pardon, sweet Father.
VINCENTIO   Lives my sweet son?
BIANCA
Pardon, dear Father.
BAPTISTA   How hast thou offended?
  Where is Lucentio?
LUCENTIO   Here's Lucentio,
Right son to the right Vincentio,
That have by marriage made thy daughter mine,
While counterfeit supposes bleared thine eyne.   110

---

88 forthcoming ready to stand trial when required   **93–94 coney-
catched** tricked   **98 wert best** might as well   **101 haled** hauled about,
maltreated   **103 spoiled** ruined   **110 supposes** suppositions, false
appearances (with an allusion to Gascoigne's *Supposes*, an adaptation of
I Suppositi by Ariosto, from which Shakespeare took the Lucentio-
Bianca plot of intrigue).   **eyne** eyes

GREMIO
  Here's packing, with a witness, to deceive us all!   111
VINCENTIO
  Where is that damnèd villain Tranio,
  That faced and braved me in this matter so?   113
BAPTISTA
  Why, tell me, is not this my Cambio?
BIANCA
  Cambio is changed into Lucentio.   115
LUCENTIO
  Love wrought these miracles. Bianca's love
  Made me exchange my state with Tranio,   117
  While he did bear my countenance in the town,   118
  And happily I have arrivèd at the last
  Unto the wishèd haven of my bliss.
  What Tranio did, myself enforced him to;
  Then pardon him, sweet Father, for my sake.
VINCENTIO I'll slit the villain's nose, that would have
  sent me to the jail.
BAPTISTA [To Lucentio] But do you hear, sir? Have you
  married my daughter without asking my good will?
VINCENTIO Fear not, Baptista, we will content you, go
  to. But I will in, to be revenged for this villainy. Exit.
BAPTISTA And I, to sound the depth of this knavery.
                                                    Exit.
LUCENTIO Look not pale, Bianca; thy father will not
  frown.   Exeunt [Lucentio and Bianca].
GREMIO
  My cake is dough, but I'll in among the rest,   132
  Out of hope of all but my share of the feast.   [Exit.] 133
KATHARINA Husband, let's follow, to see the end of
  this ado.
PETRUCHIO First kiss me, Kate, and we will.
KATHARINA What, in the midst of the street?
PETRUCHIO What, art thou ashamed of me?
KATHARINA No, sir, God forbid, but ashamed to kiss.

111 packing conspiracy **113 faced and braved** bullied and defied
115 Cambio is changed (A pun; *Cambio* in Italian means "change" or
"exchange.") **117 state** social station **118 countenance** appearance
132 My . . . dough i.e., I'm out of luck **133 Out . . . but** having hope for
nothing other than

PETRUCHIO
  Why, then let's home again. [*To Grumio.*] Come, sirrah,
    let's away.

KATHARINA
  Nay, I will give thee a kiss. [*She kisses him.*] Now pray
    thee, love, stay.

PETRUCHIO
  Is not this well? Come, my sweet Kate.
  Better once than never, for never too late.   *Exeunt.* 143

✣

5.2   *Enter Baptista, Vincentio, Gremio, the Pedant,*
        Lucentio, and Bianca; [Petruchio, Kate,
        Hortensio,] Tranio, Biondello, Grumio, and
        Widow; the servingmen with Tranio bringing in
        a banquet.

LUCENTIO
  At last, though long, our jarring notes agree,
  And time it is, when raging war is done,
  To smile at scapes and perils overblown.   3
  My fair Bianca, bid my father welcome,
  While I with selfsame kindness welcome thine.
  Brother Petruchio, sister Katharina,
  And thou, Hortensio, with thy loving widow,
  Feast with the best, and welcome to my house.
  My banquet is to close our stomachs up   9
  After our great good cheer. Pray you, sit down,   10
  For now we sit to chat as well as eat.   [*They sit.*]

PETRUCHIO
  Nothing but sit and sit, and eat and eat!

BAPTISTA
  Padua affords this kindness, son Petruchio.

PETRUCHIO
  Padua affords nothing but what is kind.

---

143 once at some time. (Cf. "better late than never.")

5.2. Location: Padua. Lucentio's house.
s.d. banquet i.e., dessert   **3 scapes** escapes, close calls   **9 stomachs**
appetites (with pun on "quarrels")   **10 our . . . cheer** i.e., the wedding
feast at Baptista's

HORTENSIO
  For both our sakes, I would that word were true.

PETRUCHIO
  Now, for my life, Hortensio fears his widow.   16

WIDOW
  Then never trust me if I be afeard.

PETRUCHIO
  You are very sensible, and yet you miss my sense:
  I mean Hortensio is afeard of you.   19

WIDOW
  He that is giddy thinks the world turns round.

PETRUCHIO
  Roundly replied.

KATHARINA   Mistress, how mean you that?   21

WIDOW   Thus I conceive by him.   22

PETRUCHIO
  Conceives by me! How likes Hortensio that?

HORTENSIO
  My widow says, thus she conceives her tale.   24

PETRUCHIO
  Very well mended. Kiss him for that, good widow.

KATHARINA
  "He that is giddy thinks the world turns round":
  I pray you, tell me what you meant by that.

WIDOW
  Your husband, being troubled with a shrew,
  Measures my husband's sorrow by his woe—   29
  And now you know my meaning.

KATHARINA
  A very mean meaning.

WIDOW   Right, I mean you.   31

---

16 fears is afraid of. (But the Widow takes the word in the sense of
"frightens"; she protests she is not at all *afeard*, frightened by Hortensio.)   **19 afeard** (Petruchio takes up the Widow's word and uses it in the
sense of "suspicious," fearful she will be untrue.)   **21 Roundly** boldly
22 Thus . . . him i.e., that's what I think of him, Petruchio. (But Petruchio takes up *conceives* in the sense of "is made pregnant.")   **24 conceives** devises (with a possible pun on *tale, tail*)   **29 Measures** judges
31 very mean contemptible. (But the Widow takes up *mean* in the sense
of "have in mind," and Kate replies in the sense of "moderate in shrewishness.")

KATHARINA
  And I am mean indeed, respecting you.   32
PETRUCHIO To her, Kate!
HORTENSIO To her, widow!
PETRUCHIO
  A hundred marks, my Kate does put her down.   35
HORTENSIO That's my office.
PETRUCHIO
  Spoke like an officer. Ha' to thee, lad!   37

                       Drinks to Hortensio.

BAPTISTA
  How likes Gremio these quick-witted folks?
GREMIO
  Believe me, sir, they butt together well.   39
BIANCA
  Head, and butt! An hasty-witted body   40
  Would say your head and butt were head and horn.   41
VINCENTIO
  Ay, mistress bride, hath that awakened you?
BIANCA
  Ay, but not frighted me. Therefore I'll sleep again.
PETRUCHIO
  Nay, that you shall not; since you have begun,
  Have at you for a bitter jest or two!   45
BIANCA
  Am I your bird? I mean to shift my bush;   46
  And then pursue me as you draw your bow.
  You are welcome all.

              Exit Bianca [with Kate and Widow].

PETRUCHIO
  She hath prevented me. Here, Signor Tranio,   49
  This bird you aimed at, though you hit her not.   50

---

32 respecting compared to   **35 marks** coins worth 13 shillings 4 pence.
put her down overcome her. (But Hortensio takes up the phrase
in a bawdy sense.)   **37 officer** (playing on Hortensio's speaking of his
office or function).   **Ha'** have, i.e., here's   **39 butt** butt heads   **40 butt**
tail, bottom   **41 head and horn** (alluding to the familiar joke about
cuckold's horns)   **45 Have at** I shall come at.   **bitter** sharp   **46 Am . . .
bush** i.e., if you mean to shoot your barbs at me, I intend to move out of
the way, as a bird would fly to another bush (with a possible bawdy
double meaning)   **49 prevented** forestalled   **50 This bird** i.e., Bianca,
whom Tranio courted (*aimed at*) in his disguise as Lucentio

Therefore a health to all that shot and missed.   51
                              [*He offers a toast.*]

TRANIO
O, sir, Lucentio slipped me like his greyhound,   52
Which runs himself and catches for his master.

PETRUCHIO
A good swift simile, but something currish.   54

TRANIO
'Tis well, sir, that you hunted for yourself;
'Tis thought your deer does hold you at a bay.   56

BAPTISTA
O ho, Petruchio! Tranio hits you now.

LUCENTIO
I thank thee for that gird, good Tranio.   58

HORTENSIO
Confess, confess, hath he not hit you here?

PETRUCHIO
'A has a little galled me, I confess;
And as the jest did glance away from me,   61
'Tis ten to one it maimed you two outright.

BAPTISTA
Now, in good sadness, son Petruchio,   63
I think thou hast the veriest shrew of all.

PETRUCHIO
Well, I say no. And therefore for assurance   65
Let's each one send unto his wife;
And he whose wife is most obedient
To come at first when he doth send for her
Shall win the wager which we will propose.

HORTENSIO
Content. What's the wager?

LUCENTIO   Twenty crowns.

PETRUCHIO   Twenty crowns!
I'll venture so much of my hawk or hound,   72
But twenty times so much upon my wife.

LUCENTIO   A hundred, then.

51 a health a toast   **52 slipped** unleashed   **54 swift** (1) quick-witted
(2) concerning swiftness.   **currish** (1) ignoble (2) concerning dogs   **56 deer**
(punning on *dear*).   **does . . . bay** turns on you like a cornered animal
and holds you at a distance   **58 gird** sharp, biting jest   **61 glance away**
ricochet off   **63 sadness** seriousness   **65 assurance** proof   **72 of** on

HORTENSIO   Content.
PETRUCHIO   A match. 'Tis done.
HORTENSIO   Who shall begin?
LUCENTIO   That will I.
  Go, Biondello, bid your mistress come to me.
BIONDELLO   I go.   *Exit.*
BAPTISTA
  Son, I'll be your half Bianca comes.   81
LUCENTIO
  I'll have no halves; I'll bear it all myself.

        Enter Biondello.

  How now, what news?
BIONDELLO
  Sir, my mistress sends you word
  That she is busy and she cannot come.
PETRUCHIO
  How? She's busy and she cannot come!
  Is that an answer?
GREMIO   Ay, and a kind one too.
  Pray God, sir, your wife send you not a worse.
PETRUCHIO   I hope better.
HORTENSIO
  Sirrah Biondello, go and entreat my wife
  To come to me forthwith.   *Exit Biondello.*
PETRUCHIO   O ho, entreat her!
  Nay, then she must needs come.
HORTENSIO   I am afraid, sir,
  Do what you can, yours will not be entreated.

        Enter Biondello.

  Now, where's my wife?
BIONDELLO
  She says you have some goodly jest in hand.
  She will not come. She bids you come to her.
PETRUCHIO
  Worse and worse. She will not come!
  O, vile, intolerable, not to be endured!
  Sirrah Grumio, go to your mistress.
  Say I command her come to me.   *Exit [Grumio].*

81 be your half take half your bet

HORTENSIO
I know her answer.
PETRUCHIO   What?
HORTENSIO   She will not.
PETRUCHIO
The fouler fortune mine, and there an end.

Enter Katharina.

BAPTISTA
Now, by my halidom, here comes Katharina!   103
KATHARINA
What is your will, sir, that you send for me?
PETRUCHIO
Where is your sister, and Hortensio's wife?
KATHARINA
They sit conferring by the parlor fire.
PETRUCHIO
Go fetch them hither. If they deny to come,
Swinge me them soundly forth unto their husbands.   108
Away, I say, and bring them hither straight.
                               [*Exit Katharina.*]
LUCENTIO
Here is a wonder, if you talk of a wonder.
HORTENSIO
And so it is. I wonder what it bodes.
PETRUCHIO
Marry, peace it bodes, and love, and quiet life,
An awful rule, and right supremacy,   113
And, to be short, what not that's sweet and happy.
BAPTISTA
Now, fair befall thee, good Petruchio!
The wager thou hast won, and I will add
Unto their losses twenty thousand crowns,
Another dowry to another daughter,
For she is changed as she had never been.   119
PETRUCHIO
Nay, I will win my wager better yet,

---

103 by my halidom (Originally an oath by the holy relics, but confused with an oath to the Virgin Mary.) **108 Swinge** thrash. **me** i.e., at my behest. (*Me* is used colloquially.) **113 awful rule** authority commanding awe or respect **119 as . . . been** as if she had never existed, i.e., she is totally changed

And show more sign of her obedience,
Her new-built virtue and obedience.

Enter Kate, Bianca, and Widow.

See where she comes, and brings your froward wives
As prisoners to her womanly persuasion.—
Katharine, that cap of yours becomes you not.
Off with that bauble. Throw it underfoot.

[*She obeys.*]

WIDOW
  Lord, let me never have a cause to sigh
  Till I be brought to such a silly pass!   128
BIANCA
  Fie, what a foolish duty call you this?
LUCENTIO
  I would your duty were as foolish too.
  The wisdom of your duty, fair Bianca,
  Hath cost me an hundred crowns since suppertime.
BIANCA
  The more fool you, for laying on my duty.   13.
PETRUCHIO
  Katharine, I charge thee tell these headstrong women
  What duty they do owe their lords and husbands.
WIDOW
  Come, come, you're mocking; we will have no telling.
PETRUCHIO
  Come on, I say, and first begin with her.
WIDOW   She shall not.
PETRUCHIO
  I say she shall—and first begin with her.
KATHARINA
  Fie, fie! Unknit that threatening unkind brow,
  And dart not scornful glances from those eyes,
  To wound thy lord, thy king, thy governor.
  It blots thy beauty as frosts do bite the meads,
  Confounds thy fame as whirlwinds shake fair buds,   144
  And in no sense is meet or amiable.
  A woman moved is like a fountain troubled,   146

128 pass state of affairs **133 laying** wagering **144 Confounds thy
fame** ruins your reputation **146 moved** angry

Muddy, ill-seeming, thick, bereft of beauty;
And while it is so, none so dry or thirsty
Will deign to sip or touch one drop of it.
Thy husband is thy lord, thy life, thy keeper,
Thy head, thy sovereign; one that cares for thee,
And for thy maintenance commits his body
To painful labor both by sea and land,
To watch the night in storms, the day in cold,
Whilst thou liest warm at home, secure and safe;
And craves no other tribute at thy hands
But love, fair looks, and true obedience—
Too little payment for so great a debt.
Such duty as the subject owes the prince,
Even such a woman oweth to her husband;
And when she is froward, peevish, sullen, sour,   161
And not obedient to his honest will,
What is she but a foul contending rebel
And graceless traitor to her loving lord?
I am ashamed that women are so simple   165
To offer war where they should kneel for peace,
Or seek for rule, supremacy, and sway
When they are bound to serve, love, and obey.
Why are our bodies soft and weak and smooth,
Unapt to toil and trouble in the world,   170
But that our soft conditions and our hearts   171
Should well agree with our external parts?
Come, come, you froward and unable worms!   173
My mind hath been as big as one of yours,   174
My heart as great, my reason haply more,
To bandy word for word and frown for frown;
But now I see our lances are but straws,
Our strength as weak, our weakness past compare,
That seeming to be most which we indeed least are.
Then vail your stomachs, for it is no boot,   180
And place your hands below your husband's foot,
In token of which duty, if he please,
My hand is ready; may it do him ease.   183

161 peevish obstinate   **165 simple** foolish   **170 Unapt** unfit   **171 conditions** qualities   **173 unable worms** i.e., poor feeble creatures   **174 big**
haughty   **180 vail your stomachs** lower your pride.   **boot** profit, use
183 do him ease give him pleasure

PETRUCHIO
  Why, there's a wench! Come on, and kiss me, Kate.
                                          [*They kiss.*]
LUCENTIO
  Well, go thy ways, old lad, for thou shalt ha 't.
VINCENTIO
  'Tis a good hearing when children are toward.   186
LUCENTIO
  But a harsh hearing when women are froward.
PETRUCHIO   Come, Kate, we'll to bed.
  We three are married, but you two are sped.   189
  [*To Lucentio.*] 'Twas I won the wager, though you hit the
     white,   190
  And, being a winner, God give you good night!
                                Exit Petruchio [*and Kate*].

HORTENSIO
  Now, go thy ways, thou hast tamed a curst shrew.   192
LUCENTIO
  'Tis a wonder, by your leave, she will be tamed so.
                                          [*Exeunt.*]

---

186 'Tis . . . toward i.e., one likes to hear when children are obedient
189 We . . . sped i.e., all we three men have taken wives, but you two are
done for (*sped*) through disobedient wives   **190 the white** the center of
the target (with quibble on the name of Bianca, which in Italian means
"white")   **192 shrew** pronounced "shrow" (and thus spelled in the
Folio). See also 4.1.198 and 5.2.28.

Date and Text

The Taming of the Shrew was not printed until the First Folio of 1623. Francis Meres does not mention the play in 1598 in his *Palladis Tamia: Wit's Treasury* (a slender volume on contemporary literature and art; valuable because it lists most of Shakespeare's plays that existed at that time), unless it is the mysterious *"Loue labours wonne"* on his list. (Meres is not totally accurate, for he omits *Henry VI* from the history plays.) The play must have existed prior to 1598, however, for its style is comparable with that of *The Two Gentlemen of Verona* and other early comedies. Moreover, a play called *The Taming of A Shrew* appeared in print in 1594 (Stationers' Register, May 1594). The relationship of that text to Shakespeare's play is problematic, and several theories prevail. One is that *A Shrew* represents a source for Shakespeare's play, or even an early version by Shakespeare. If, as seems more likely, *A Shrew* is later, then it may be an imitation by some rival dramatist, who relied chiefly on his memory and who changed characters' names and the location to make the play seem his. More probably, it is a somewhat uncharacteristic kind of reported or "bad" quarto, reconstructed and "improved" upon by a writer who also borrowed admiringly from Christopher Marlowe and other Elizabethan dramatists. In either case, Shakespeare's play would have to be dated earlier than May 1594.

The title page of *A Shrew* proclaims that "it was sundry times acted by the *Right honorable the Earle of* Pembrook his seruants." Quite possibly this derivative version was merely trying to capitalize on the original's stage success and was in fact describing performances of Shakespeare's play. Theater owner and manager Philip Henslowe's record of a performance of *"the Tamynge of A Shrowe"* in 1594 at Newington Butts, a mile south of London Bridge, may also refer to Shakespeare's play; certainly the minute distinction between "A Shrew" and "The Shrew" is one that the official records of the time would overlook. The Admiral's men and the Lord Chamberlain's men, acting companies, were playing at Newington Butts at the time, either jointly or alternatingly. Since Shakespeare's company, the Chamberlain's, later owned *The Shrew*, they may well have owned and acted it on this occasion in 1594, having obtained it from the Earl of Pembroke's men when that company disbanded in 1593. Many of Pembroke's leading players joined the Chamberlain's, Shakespeare quite possibly among them. (The possibility that he came to the Chamberlain's from Lord Strange's men seems less certain today than it once did.) It is entirely possible, then, that *The Shrew* was acted by Pembroke's men in 1592–1593 and subsequently passed along to the Chamberlain's.

The Folio text of this play is now generally thought to have been printed from Shakespeare's working manuscript or possibly from a transcript incorporating some minor theatrical changes.

Textual Notes

These textual notes are not a historical collation, either of the early folios or of more recent editions; they are simply a record of departures in this edition from the copy text. The reading adopted in this edition appears in boldface, followed by the rejected reading from the copy text, i.e., the First Folio. Only major alterations in punctuation are noted. Changes in lineation are not indicated, nor are some minor and obvious typographical errors.

Abbreviations used:
F the First Folio
s.d. stage direction
s.p. speech prefix

Copy Text: The First Folio.

Ind.1. s.d. Christopher Sly [printed at the end of the s.d. in F]   **1 s.p. [and elsewhere] Sly** Begger   **10–11 thirdborough** Headborough   **16 Breathe** Brach   **21 s.p. [and elsewhere] First Huntsman** Hunts   **81 s.p. First Player** 2. Player   **87 s.p. Second Player** Sincklo   **99 s.p. First Player** Plai **134 peasant.** peasant,

Ind.2. 2 lordship Lord   **18 Sly's** Sies   **26 s.p. [and elsewhere] Third Servant** 3 Man   **27 s.p. [and elsewhere] Second Servant** 2 Man   **47 s.p. [and elsewhere] First Servant** 1 Man   **53 wi' th'** with   **99 s.p. [and elsewhere] Page** Lady   **125 s.p. Servant** Mes   **133 it. Is** it is

1.1. 13 Vincentio Vincentio's   **14 brought** brough   **24 satiety** sacietie   **25 Mi perdonate** Me Pardonato   **47 s.d. suitor** sister   **57 s.p. [and elsewhere] Katharina** Kate   **146 s.d. Manent** Manet   **163 captum** captam   **208 colored** Conlord   **227 time.** time   **244 your** you   **248 s.d. speak** speakes

1.2. 17 s.d. wrings rings   **18 masters** mistris   **24 Con . . . trovato** Contutti le core bene trobatto   **25 ben** bene   **26 Molto** multo   **onorato** honorata **33 pip** peepe   **45 this's** this   **51 grows. But** growes but   **72 she** she is **120 me and other** me. Other   **171 help me** helpe one   **189 Antonio's** Butonios   **212 ours** yours   **265 feat** seeke   **280 ben** Been

2.1. 8 thee, tell tel   **79 unto you** vnto   **104 Pisa. By** Pisa by   **153 struck** stroke   **157 rascal fiddler** Rascall, fidler   **168 s.d. Exeunt** Exit   **186 bonny** bony   **244 askance** a sconce   **322 s.d. Exeunt** Exit   **328 in me** me   **352 Valance** Vallens   **355 pail** pale   **373 Marseilles'** Marcellus

3.1. 28 Sigeia sigeria [also at ll. 33 and 42]   **43 steterat** staterat   **47 [Aside]** Luc   **50 s.p. Bianca** [not in F]   **51 s.p. Lucentio** Bian   **53 s.p. Bianca** Hort **76 clef** Cliffe   **80 change** charge   **odd** old   **81 s.p. Servant** Nicke

3.2. 29 of thy of   **30 old news** newes   **33 hear** heard   **54 swayed** Waid **56 cheeked** chekt   **130 As I As** As   **150 e'er** ere   **199 s.p. Gremio** Gra

4.1. 23 s.p. Curtis Gru   **42 their white** the white   **81 sleekly** slickely **106 s.p. Grumio** Gre   **136 off** of   **168 s.d. Curtis** Curtis a Seruant [after l. 169 in F]

4.2. 4 s.p. Hortensio Luc **6 s.p. Lucentio** Hor [and at l. 8] **13 none** me
31 her them **72 Take . . . alone** [assigned to "Par." in F] **in** me

4.3. [F has "Actus Quartus. Scena Prima" here] **63 s.p. Haberdasher** Fel
81 is a is **88 like a** like **146 where,** where **177 account'st** accountedst

4.4. s.d. [booted] [appears at l. 18 in F] **1 Sir** Sirs **5 Where . . . Pegasus**
[assigned to Tranio in F] **68** [F adds a s.d.: "Enter Peter"] **91 except**
expect

4.5. 18 is in **35 make a** make the **37 where** whether **77 she be** she

5.1. 4. [F has "Exit" here] **6 master's** mistris **42 brought** brough
50 master's Mistris **104 s.d. Exeunt** Exit **139 No** Mo **143 than never**
then ueuer
5.2. [F has "Actus Quintus" here] **2 done** come **37 thee** the **45 bitter**
better **two** too **52 s.p. Tranio** Tri **57 ho** oh **62 two** too **65 for** sir
132 an fiue **136 you're** your

Shakespeare's Sources

Most recent critics agree that the play called *The Taming of a Shrew*, published in 1594, is derived from a now-lost earlier version of Shakespeare's play to which the compiler added original material and borrowed or even plagiarized from other literary sources as well. It does not, then, appear to be a source for Shakespeare's play as Geoffrey Bullough has argued in his *Narrative and Dramatic Sources of Shakespeare* (1966). Apart from this question, all critics agree that Shakespeare's play consists of three elements, each with its own source: the romantic love plot of Lucentio and Bianca, the wife-taming plot of Petruchio and Kate, and the framing plot or, induction, of Christopher Sly.

The romantic love plot is derived from George Gascoigne's *Supposes*, a neoclassical comedy performed at Gray's Inn (one of the Inns of Court, where young men studied law in London) in 1566. Gascoigne's play was a rather close translation of Lodovico Ariosto's *I Suppositi* (1509), which in turn was based on two classical plays, Terence's *Eunuchus* and Plautus' *Captivi*. The heroine of Gascoigne's version (as of Ariosto's) is Polynesta, the resourceful daughter of Damon, a widower of Ferrara. Two suitors vie for Polynesta's hand: Dr. Cleander, an aged and miserly lawyer, and Erostrato, a Sicilian gentleman who has purportedly come to Ferrara to study. In fact, however, this "Erostrato" is the servant Dulippo in disguise, having changed places with his master. (These disguisings are the "supposes" of the title.) As a servant in Damon's household, "Dulippo" has secretly become the lover of Polynesta and has made her pregnant. Balia, the nurse, or duenna, is their go-between. Meanwhile, "Erostrato" takes great delight in outwitting Dr. Cleander and his unattractive parasite, Pasiphilo. The counterfeit Erostrato's ruse is to produce a rich father who will guarantee a handsome dowry and thereby outbid Cleander in the contest for Polynesta's hand. The "father" he produces, however, is actually an old Sienese stranger, who is persuaded that he is in danger in Ferrara unless he cloaks his identity. Complications arise when Damon learns of his daughter's affair and throws the

lover, "Dulippo," into a dungeon. The crafty Pasiphilo over-
hears this compromising information and resolves to cause
mischief for all the principals. Moreover, when Erostrato's
real father, Philogano, arrives in Ferrara, he is barred from
his son's house by the counterfeit Philogano and resolves to
get help. His clever servant, Litio, suggests employing the
famous lawyer Cleander. All is happily resolved when the
real Dulippo proves to be the son of Dr. Cleander, and
the real Erostrato is revealed to be rich and socially eligible
for Polynesta's hand in marriage. Cleander is even recon-
ciled to his parasite, Pasiphilo.

Shakespeare, in his play, has almost entirely eliminated
the satire of the law that is in his source. Gremio is aged
and wealthy, but no shyster. The lover is not imprisoned in a
dungeon. The parasite is gone, as also in *The Comedy of Errors*. Bianca does not consummate her affair with Lucentio
as does Polynesta, and hence has no need for a go-between
like Balia. Shakespeare adapts a sophisticated neoclassical
comedy, racy and cosmopolitan, to the moral standards of
his public theater. The witless Hortensio, the tutoring in
Latin, and the music lesson are Shakespeare's invention.

The wife-taming plot of Petruchio and Kate reflects an
ancient comic misogynistic tradition, still extant today in
the Scottish folksong "The Cooper of Fife" or "The Wife
Wrapped in Wether's Skin" (Francis James Child, *The English and Scottish Popular Ballads* [1888–1898], 5:104). Richard Hosley has argued (in *Huntington Library Quarterly* 27,
1964) that Shakespeare's likeliest source was *A Merry Jest
of a Shrewd and Curst Wife Lapped in Morel's Skin, for her
Good Behavior* (printed c. 1550). Excerpts of this ballad follow. In this version, the husband beats his shrewish wife
with birch rods until she bleeds and faints, whereupon he
wraps her in the raw salted skin of an old plow-horse
named Morel. Like Kate, this shrewish wife has a gentle
younger sister who is their father's favorite. This father
warns the man who proposes to marry his older daughter
that she is shrewish, but the suitor goes ahead and subsequently tames his wife with Morel's skin. Thereafter, at a
celebratory dinner, everyone is impressed by the thorough-
ness of the taming.

Shakespeare avoids the misogynistic extremes of this
story, despite the similarity of the narrative. Instead, he

seems to have had in mind the more humanistic spirit of Erasmus's *A Merry Dialogue Declaring the Properties of Shrewd Shrews and Honest Wives* (translated 1557) and Juan Luis Vives's *The Office and Duty of an Husband* (translated 1555). Specific elements of the wife-taming plot have been traced to other possible sources. The scolding of a tailor occurs in Gerard Legh's *Accidence of Armory* (1562); a wife agrees with her husband's assertion of a patent falsehood in Don Juan Manuel's *El Conde Lucanor* (1335); and three husbands wager on the obedience of their wives in *The Book of the Knight of La Tour-Landry* (printed 1484).

The induction story, of the beggar duped into believing himself a rich lord, is an old tale occurring in the *Arabian Nights*. An interesting analogue occurs in P. Heuterus's *De Rebus Burgundicis* (1584), translated into the French of S. Goulart (1606?) and thence into the English of Edward Grimeston (1607). According to Heuterus, in 1440 Philip the Good of Burgundy actually entertained a drunken beggar in his palace "to make trial of the vanity of our life," plying him with fine clothes, bed, a feast, and the performance of "a pleasant comedy."

A Merry Jest
of a Shrewd and Curst Wife
Lapped in Morel's Skin

Listen, friends, and hold you still;
Abide awhile and dwell.
A merry jest tell you I will,
And how that it befell.
As I went walking upon a day
Among my friends to sport,
To an house I took the way
To rest me for my comfort.

A great feast was kept there then,
And many one was thereat,
With wives and maidens and many a good man
That made good game and chat.

Title: Shrewd shrewish

It befell then at that tide   13
An honest man was there;
A cursèd dame sat by his side
That often did him dere.   16

His wife she was, I tell you plain,
This dame, ye may me trow.   18
To play the master she would not lain   19
And make her husband bow.
At every word that she did speak
To be peace he was full fain,   22
Or else she would take him on the cheek   23
Or put him to other pain.

When she did wink, he durst not stir   25
Nor play wherever he went
With friend or neighbor to make good cheer,
When she her brows bent.
These folk had two maidens fair and free   29
Which were their daughters dear.
This is true, believe you me:
Of conditions was none their peer.   32

The youngest was meek and gentle, iwis;   33
Her father's condition she had.
The eldest her mother's, withouten miss: 35
Sometimes frantic and sometimes mad.   36
The father had his pleasure in the one alway,
And glad he was her to behold;
The mother in the other, this is no nay,   39
For in all her curstness she made her bold.   40

And at the last she was, in fay,   41
As curst as her mother in word and deed   42
Her mischievous pageants sometime to play,   43
Which caused her father's heart to bleed.

---

13 tide time **16 dere** vex **18 trow** believe **19 lain** i.e., disguise her ambi-
tion **22 be peace** be silent. **full fain** very willing **23 take him** give him a
blow **25 wink** close or avert her eye **29 free** of good breeding **32 conditions** quality, nature **33 iwis** certainly **35 withouten miss** without doubt
36 frantic ungovernable. **mad** angry **39 no nay** certain **40 in all . . . bold**
i.e., the mother encouraged her shrewishness in every way **41 at the last**
in sum. **in fay** in good faith **42 curst** shrewish **43 Her . . . play** i.e.,
playing her mischievous tricks

For he was woe and nothing glad,   45
And of her would fain be rid.
He wished to God that some man her had,
But yet to marriage he dust her not bid.

Full many there came the youngest to have,
But her father was loath her to forgo.
None there came the eldest to crave
For fear it should turn them to woe.
The father was loath any man to beguile,   54
For he was true and just withal.
Yet there came one within a while
That her demanded in the hall.

[The meek and gentle younger daughter is quickly wooed
and wedded; the father grieves to lose her, but the mother is
only too glad to get rid of her. When a suitor to the shrewish
elder daughter shows up, much to the father's surprise, the
kind old man warns of the danger: this daughter has been
taught by her mother "to be master of her husband." The
young man persists nonetheless and wins the mother's consent to the match. The mother advises him to pay heed to
his wife's wishes if he wants to enjoy domestic harmony—
especially since the wife will bring with her a considerable
dowry. The young man is not wealthy but is a good craftsman and willing to work hard. The wife-to-be gives him
plain notice of her intention to rule the roost in marriage,
but he has his own plans about that; he knows he is marrying a woman with a "proud heart," but one who will in all
events bring with her "an heap of gold."

And so the wedding takes place, followed by a wedding
feast with much giving of gifts (including a hundred pounds
to set the bridegroom up in his chosen craft), and dancing.
The wedding night appears to be a success, the new husband playing with his wife "Even as the cat was wont with
the mouse." Their sparring begins on the very next morning, as husband and wife lie abed while the bride's mother
prepares them a caudle, a warm drink of gruel and wine.]

When that the mother departed was,

---

45 woe woeful.   **nothing** not at all   **54 withal** in addition

They dallied together and had good game.
He hit her awry. She cried, "Alas!
What do ye, man? Hold up, for shame!"   514
"I will, sweet wife," then gan he say,
"Fulfill your mind, both loud and still.   516
But ye be able, I swear in fay,   517
In all sports to abide my will."

And they wrestled so long beforn
That this they had for their great meed: 520
Both shirt and smock was all to-torne,   521
That their uprising had no speed.   522
But yet the mother came again
And said to her daughter, "How dost thou now?"
"Marry, mother, between us twain
Our shirts be torn, I make God a vow.

"By God's dear mother," she sware then,
"This order with us may not continue.   528
I will no more lie by this man,
For he doth me brast both vein and sinew.   530
Nay, nay, dear mother, this world goeth on wheels.   531
By sweet Saint George, ye may me trow:
He lieth kicking with his heels   533
That he is like to bear me a blow."   534

[The newlyweds get past this difficulty and join their
friends in the hall for the caudle and more celebration.
Even the father's apprehensions are quieted to a degree,
and parents and friends leave the happy couple to their new
household. The husband sets up his shop "with haberdash
ware," i.e., petty merchandise, and bestows great care on
his plows and livestock as well. Trouble next erupts when
the farm laborers who tend his cattle and sheep come in
from the field for their meal only to be greeted by a burst of
shrewish temper from their new mistress.]

514 **Hold up** stop   516 **Fulfill** satisfy the desire of   517 **in fay** in good
faith   520 **meed** reward   521 **to-torne** torn to bits   522 **their . . . speed** they
were in no hurry to get out of bed   528 **order** i.e., condition of matri-
mony   530 **me brast . . . sinew** i.e., bursts asunder my blood vessels and
tendons   531 **goeth on wheels** goes on its own way (i.e., this too will
pass)   533 **kicking with his heels** i.e., flat on his back   534 **That . . .
bear me** he that is likely to receive from me

With countenance grim and words smart 607
She gave them meat and bade them brast. 608
The poor folk that come from plow and cart
Of her lewd words they were aghast, 610
Saying each to other, "What dame is this?
The devil I trow hath brought us here. 612
Our master shall know it, by heaven's bliss,
That we will not serve him another year."

The goodman was forth in the town abroad 615
About other things, I you say.
When he came homeward, he met with a goad: 617
One of his carters was going away.
To whom he said, "Lob, whither goest thou?"
The carter spied his master then,
And said to him, "I make God a vow,
No longer with thy wife abide I can.

"Master," he said, "by God's blist, 623
Our dame is the devil, thou mayst me believe!
If thou have sought her, thou hast not missed 625
Of one that full often thee shall grieve. 626
By God, a man thou canst not have
To go to cart ne yet to plow, 628
Neither boy nor yet knave,
By God's dear mother, I make God a vow,

"That will bide with thee day or night.
Our dame is not for us, for she doth curse.
When we shall eat or drink with right, 633
She bans and frowns, that we be all the worse. 634
We be not used, wherever we wend,
To be sorely looked on for eating of our meat. 636
The devil I trow is to thee send. 637
God help us a better mistress to get!"

"Come on thy way, Lob, and turn again.
Go home with me and all shall be well.

607 smart stinging **608 brast** stuff themselves until they burst **610 lewd** rude **612 brought us** i.e., brought her to us **615 goodman** yeoman, householder **617 goad** i.e., sting, annoyance **623 blist** bliss **625-626 If . . . grieve** i.e., if you chose her, you picked one that will grieve you very often **628 ne** nor **633 shall** wish to **634 bans** curses **636 sorely looked on** harshly regarded **637 is to thee send** has been sent to you

An ox for my meiny shall be slain   641
And the hide at the market I will sell."
Upon this together home they went.
The goodman was angry in his mind,
But yet to his wife with good intent
He said, "Sweetheart, ye be unkind.

"Entreat our meiny well alway,   647
And give them meat and drink enough,
For they get our living every day,   649
And theirs also, at cart and plough.
Therefore I would that they should have
Meat and drink to their behoof.   652
For, my sweet wife, so God me save,
Ye will do so, if ye me love."

"Give them what thou wilt! I do not care,
By day and night, man, believe thou me.
Whatever they have, or how they fare,
I pray God evil mote they thee.   658
And specially that whoreson that doth complain.
I will quit him once, if ever I live!   660
I will dash the knave upon the brain
That ever after it shall him grieve."

"What, my dear wife? For shame, be still.
This is a pain, such words to hear.
We cannot always have our will,
Though that we were a king's peer.
For, to shame a knave, what can they get?   667
Thou art as lewd, 'fore God, as they.   668
And therefore shalt thou serve them of meat
And drink also, from hence alway.   670

"What, wife? Ye be to blame
To speak to me thus in this wise.
If we should strive, folk would speak shame.
Therefore be still, in mine advice.
I am loath with you to strive,

641 meiny retinue, company **647 Entreat** treat **649 get** earn **652 behoof**
use, benefit **658 mote they thee** may they thrive **660 quit** repay **667 For**
. . . **get** i.e., what good does it do to scorn someone who is below you in
social station (?) or, you should be ashamed; what can they get on their
own **668 lewd** rude, ill-mannered **670 hence** henceforth. **alway** always

For aught that you shall do or say.
I swear to Christ, wife, by my life,
I had rather take Morel and ride my way

To seek mine adventure till your mood be past.
I say to you, these manners be not good.
Therefore, I pray you that this be the last
Of your furious anger that seemeth so wood.   682
What can it avail you me for to grieve
That loveth you so well as I do, mine heart?
By my troth, wife, you may me believe,
Such toys as these be would make us both smart."   686

"Smart, in the twenty feigning devils' name!
That list me once well for to see.   688
I pray God give thee evil shame.
What shouldest thou be, wert it not for me?   690
A rag on thine arse thou shouldst not have
Except my friends had given it thee.   692
Therefore I tell thee well, thou drunken knave,
Thou art not he that shall rule me."

"O good wife, cease and let this overpass,
For all your great anger and high words eke.   696
I am mine own self even as I was,
And to you will be loving and also meek.
But if ye should do thus as ye do begin,
It may not continue no time, iwis.
I would not let, for kith nor kin,   701
To make you mend all things that is amiss."

"Make me? Marry, out upon thee, drivel!   703
Sayest thou that, wilt thou begin?
I pray God and Our Lady that a foul evil
Lighten upon thee and all thy kin!   706
By God's dear blist, vex me no more,   707
For if thou do thou shalt repent.
I have yet something for thee in store."
And with that a staff in her hand she hent.   710

682 wood furious, mad   **686 toys** antics   **688 That . . . see** I'd really like to
see that   **690 What shouldest thou be** where would you be, what kind of
life would you have   **692 friends** relatives   **696 eke** also   **701 let** hesitate.
kith friends and neighbors   **703 drivel** drudge, imbecile   **706 Lighten**
alight   **707 blist** bliss   **710 hent** seized

At him full soon then she let flee,
And whirled about her as it had been a man.
Her husband then was fain, perdy,   713
To void her stroke and go his way then.   714
"By God's dear mother!" then gan she swear,
"From henceforth I will make thee bow.
For I will trim thee in thy gear,
Or else I would I were called a sow.

"Fie on all wretches that be like thee,
In word or work, both loud and still!
I swear by Him that made man free,
Of me thou shalt not have thy will,
Now nor never, I tell thee plain;
For I will have gold and riches enow
When thou shalt go jagged as a simple swain   725
With whip in hand at cart and plow."

"Of that, my dear wife, I take no scorn,
For many a goodman with mind and heart
Hath gone to plow and cart beforn
My time, iwis, with pain and smart,
Which now be rich and have good will,
Being at home, and make good cheer,
And there they intend to lead their life still
Till our Lord do send for them here.   734

"But now I must ride a little way,
Dear wife. I will come right soon again.
Appoint our dinner, I you pray,   737
For I do take on me great pain.
I do my best, I swear by my life,
To order you like a woman, iwis,
And yet it cannot be withouten strife,
Through your lewd tongue, by heaven's bliss."

"Ride to the devil and to his dame!
I would I should thee never see.
I pray God send thee mickle shame   745
In any place wherever thou be.
Thou wouldest fain the master play,

---

713 fain, perdy glad, by God **714 void** avoid **725 jagged** i.e., in jagged, tat-
tered clothes **734 here** i.e., on earth **737 Appoint** prepare **745 mickle** much

But thou shalt not, by God I make thee sure!
I swear I will thy petticoat pay,   749
That long with me thou shalt not endure."

[The husband rides away, musing on his misfortune and re-
penting that he ever married but blaming no one but himself. He vows to make his wife regret her behavior by
beating her until she is black and blue and groaning for
woe. Nothing will do, he perceives, except to wrap her in the
skin of Morel, a faithful horse that has long drawn the plow
and the cart but is now old and infirm. Having resolved on
this course of action, he returns home to see what kind of
welcome he will get.]

"Where art thou, wife? Shall I have any meat?
Or am I not so welcome unto thee
That at my commandment I shall aught get?
I pray thee heartily soon tell thou me.
If thou do not serve me, and that anon,   843
I shall thee show mine anger, iwis.
I swear by God and by Saint John
Thy bones will I swaddle, so have I bliss."   846

Forth she came, as breme as a boar,   847
And like a dog she rated him then,   848
Saying thus: "I set no store   849
By thee, thou wretch! Thou art no man.
Get thee hence out of my sight,
For meat nor drink thou gettest none here.
I swear to thee, by Mary bright,
Of me thou gettest here no good cheer."

"Well, wife," he said, "thou dost me compel
To do that thing that I were loath.
If I bereave Morel of his old fell   857
Thou shalt repent it, by the faith now goeth.   858

---

749 thy petticoat pay flog your waistcoat (with you in it); i.e., I will make
you pay for this

843 anon at once **846 straddle** beat soundly **847 breme** fierce **848 rated**
scolded **849–850 set no store By thee** esteem you of no value **857 fell**
skin **858 by the faith now goeth** by the faith of Christians nowadays;
i.e., that's for sure

For I see well that it will no better be   859
But in it thou must, after the new guise.   860
It had been better, so mote I thee,   861
That thou haddest not begun this enterprise.

"Now will I begin my wife to tame,
That all the world shall it know.
I would be loath her for to shame,
Though she do not care, ye may me trow.   866
Yet will I her honesty regard
And it preserve wherever ye may.   868
But Morel, that is in yonder yard,
His hide therefore he must leese, in fay."   870

And so he commanded anon
To slay old Morel, his great horse,
And flay him then the skin from the bone
To wrap it about his wife's white corse.
Also he commanded of a birchen tree   875
Rods to be made a good great heap,
And sware, by dear God in Trinity
His wife in his cellar should skip and leap.

"The hide must be salted," then he said eke,   879
"Because I would not have it stink.
I hope herewith she will be meek,
For this I trow will make her shrink
And bow at my pleasure when I her bed,
And obey my commandments both loud and still,
Or else I will make her body bleed
And with sharp rods beat her my fill."

Anon with that to her he gan to call.
She bid, "Abide, in the devil's name!
I will not come, whatso befall.
Sit still, with sorrow and mickle shame.
Thou shalt not rule me as pleaseth thee,
I will well thou know, by God's dear mother;   892
But thou shalt be ruled alway by me,

859–860 it will . . . must there is nothing else for it but that you must go
into it   861 so mote I thee as I hope to prosper   866 Though even
though. me trow believe me   868 wherever ye may wherever I
may (?)   870 leese lose. in fay in good faith   875 birchen birch
879 eke also   892 I will I wish

And I will be master and none other."

"Wilt thou be master, dear wife? In fay,
Then must we wrestle for the best game.
If thou it win, then may I say
That I have done myself great shame.
But first I will make thee sweat, good Joan,   899
Red blood even to the heels a-down,
And lap thee in Morel's skin alone,   901
That the blood shall be seen even from the crown."

"Sayest thou me that, thou wretched knave?
It were better thou haddest me never seen!
I swear to thee, so God me save,
With my nails I will scratch out both thine eyen.   906
And therefore think not to touch me once,
For, by the Mass, if thou begin that,
Thou shalt be handled for the nonce   909
That all thy brains on the ground shall squat."

"Why, then, there is no remedy, I see,
But needs I must do even as I thought.
Seeing it will none otherwise be,
I will thee not spare, by God that me bought!   914
For now I am set thee for to charm   915
And make thee meek, by God's might,
Or else with rods, while thou art warm,
I shall thee scourge with reason and right.

"Now will I my sweet wife trim,
According as she deserveth to me.   920
I swear by God and by Saint Sim
With birchen rods well beat shall she be.
And after that, in Morel's salt skin
I will her lay and full fast bind,
That all her friends and eke her kin
Shall her long seek or they her find."   926

Then he her met, and to her gan say,
"How sayest thou, wife, wilt thou be master yet?"
She sware by God's body, and by that day,
And suddenly with her fist she did him hit,

899 sweat i.e., bleed **901 lap** enwrap **906 eyen** eyes **909 for the
nonce** i.e., in such a way **914 bought** redeemed **915 charm** subdue
920 to me at my hands **926 or** ere

And defied him, drivel, at every word,   931
Saying, "Precious whoreson, what dost thou think?   932
I set not by thee a stinking turd.   933
Thou shalt get of me neither meat nor drink."

"Sayest thou me that, wife?" quoth he then.
With that, in his arms he gan her catch.
Straight to the cellar with her he ran,
And fastened the door with lock and latch
And threw the key down him beside,
Asking her then if she would obey.
Then she said, "Nay, for all thy pride,"
But she was master and would abide alway.   942

"Then," quoth he, "we must make a fray."
And with that her clothes he gan to tear.
"Out upon thee, whoreson!" then she did say,
"Wilt thou rob me of all my gear?
It cost thee naught, thou arrant thief!"   947
And quickly she gat him by the head.
With that she said, "God give thee a mischief,
And them that fed thee first with bread!"   950

They wrestled together thus, they two,
So long that the clothes asunder went,
And to the ground he threw her tho,   953
That clean from the back her smock he rent.
In every hand a rod he gat   955
And laid upon her a right good pace,
Asking of her, "What game was that?"
And she cried out, "Whoreson! Alas! Alas!

"What wilt thou do? Wilt thou kill me?
I have made thee, a man of naught.   960
Thou shalt repent it, by God's pity,
That ever this deed thou hast y-wrought!"   962
"I care not for that, dame," he did say.

---

931 defied him, drivel scorned him as an imbecile (?)   **932 Precious whoreson** i.e., worthless rogue   **933 I set . . . turd** i.e., I don't give a turd for you
942 But she i.e., but said that she   **947 It cost thee naught** i.e., you didn't pay for it (having had no money when you married me)   **950 them . . . bread** i.e., those who raised you   **953 tho** then   **955 every hand** both hands.   **gat** got, held   **960 I . . . naught** i.e., I and my family made you what you are from a mere nobody   **962 y-wrought** done

"Thou shalt give over, or we depart,   964
The mastership all, or all this day
I will not cease to make thee smart."

Ever he laid on, and ever she did cry,
"Alas! Alas, that ever I was born!
Out on thee, murderer, I thee defy!
Thou hast my white skin and my body all to-torne!   970
Leave off betime, I counsel thee."   971
"Nay, by God, dame, I say not so yet.
I swear to thee, by Mary so free,   973
We begin but now. This is the first fit.   974

"Once again we must dance about,
And then thou shalt rest in Morel's skin."
He gave her then so many a great clout   977
That on the ground the blood was seen.
Within a while he cried, "New rods, new!"
With that she cried full loud, "Alas!"
"Dance yet about, dame; thou came not where it grew." 981
And suddenly with that in a swoon she was.

He spied that, and up he her hent   983
And wrang her hard then by the nose.   984
With her to Morel's skin straight he went
And therein full fast he did her close.   986
Within a while she did revive,
Through the gross salt that did her smart.
She thought she should never have gone on live   989
Out of Morel's skin, so sore is her heart.

When she did spy that therein she lay,   991
Out of her wit she was full nigh,
And to her husband then did she say,
"How canst thou do this villainy?"
"Nay, how sayest thou, thou cursèd wife?
In this foul skin I will thee keep

---

964 or we depart ere we part, before we're done   **970 to-torne** torn to pieces
971 betime quickly   **973 free** excellent, magnanimous   **974 fit** section of a
poem or song (i.e., we've just begun)   **977 clout** blow   **981 thou came . . .
grew** i.e., you've just started, you've had only a taste of what I have in store
for you   **983 hent** seized   **984 wrang** wrung, pinched. (Wringing by the nose
is a procedure for bringing a person to consciousness.)   **986 fast** securely
989 on live alive   **991 that therein she lay** what she was lying in

During the time of all thy life,
Therein forever to wail and weep."

With that her mood began to sink,
And said, "Dear husband, for grace I call!
For I shall never sleep or wink   1001
Till I get your love, whatso befall;
And I will never to you offend,
In no manner of wise, of all my life,   1004
Nor to do nothing that may pretend   1005
To displease you with my wits five.

"For father, nor mother, whatsoever they say,
I will not anger you, by God in throne,
But glad will your commandments obey
In presence of people and eke alone."
"Well, on that condition thou shalt have
Grace, and fair bed to rest thy body in.
But if thou rage more, so God me save,
I will wrap thee again in Morel's skin."

Then he took her out in his arms twain
And beheld her so piteously with blood arrayed.
"How thinkest thou, wife, shall we again
Have such business more?" to her he said.
She answered, "Nay, my husband dear.
While I you know and you know me,
Your commandments I will, both far and near,
Fulfill alway in every degree."

"Well, then, I promise thee, by God, even now,
Between thee and me shall never be strife.
If thou to my commandments quickly bow
I will thee cherish all the days of my life."
In bed she was laid, and healed full soon
As fair and clear as she was beforn.
What he her bid was quickly done.
To be diligent, iwis, she took no scorn.   1030

Then was he glad and thought in his mind,
"Now have I done myself great good,
And her also, we shall it find,

1001 wink close the eyes   **1004 of** during   **1005 pretend** undertake, presume   **1030 To . . . scorn** she thought it no indignity to be diligent, certainly

Though I have shed part of her blood.
For, as methink she will be meek,
Therefore I will her father and mother
Bid to guest, now the next week,   1037
And of our neighbors many other."

Great pain he made his wife to take
Against the day that they should come.   1040
Of them was none that there did lack,
I dare well say unto my doom.   1042
Yea, father and mother and neighbors all
Did thither come to make good cheer.
Soon they were set in general,   1045
The wife was diligent, as did appear.

Father and mother was welcome then,
And so were they all, in good fay.
The husband sat there like a man;   1049
The wife did serve them all that day.
The goodman commanded what he would have;
The wife was quick at hand.
"What now?" thought the mother. "This arrant knave
Is master, I understand.

"What may this mean," then she gan think,
"That my daughter so diligent is?
Now can I neither eat nor drink
Till I it know, by heaven bliss."
When her daughter came again
To serve at the board as her husband bade,
The mother stared with her eyen twain   1061
Even as one that had been mad.

All the folk that at the board sat
Did her behold then, everychone.   1064
The mother from the board her gat,   1065
Following her daughter, and that anon,
And in the kitchen she her fand,   1067
Saying unto her in this wise:

1037 **Bid to guest** invite as guests   1040 **Against** in anticipation of
1042 **unto my doom** on pain of divine judgment   1045 **Soon** as soon
as   1049 **like a man** i.e., like the man of the household   1061 **eyen**
eyes   1064 **everychone** everyone   1065 **from the board her gat** got
herself up from the table   1067 **fand** found

"Daughter, thou shalt well understand
I did not teach thee after this guise."

"Ah, good mother, ye say full well.
All things with me is not as ye ween.   1072
If ye had been in Morel's fell
As well as I, it should be seen."   1074
"In Morel's fell! What devil is that?"   1075
"Marry, mother, I will it you show.
But beware that you come not thereat,   1077
Lest you yourself then do beshrew.   1078

"Come down now in this cellar so deep
And Morel's skin there shall you see,
With many a rod that hath made me to weep,
When the blood ran down fast by my knee."
The mother this beheld and cried out, "Alas!"
And ran out of the cellar as she had been wood.   1084
She came to the table where the company was
And said, "Out, whoreson! I will see thy heart blood."   1086

"Peace, good mother! Or, so have I bliss,   1087
Ye must dance else as did my wife,
And in Morel's skin lie, that well salted is,
Which you should repent all the days of your life."
All they that were there held with the young man   1091
And said he did well in every manner degree.
When dinner was done, they departed all then;
The mother no lenger durst there be.   1094

The father abode last and was full glad,
And gave his children his blessing, iwis,
Saying the young man full well done had,
And merrily departed withouten miss.   1098
This young man was glad, ye may be sure,
That he had brought his wife to this.
God give us all grace in rest to endure,
And hereafter to come unto his bliss!

1072 **ween** think   1074 **it should be seen** i.e., you would understand
1075 **What devil** i.e., what in the devil   1077–1078 **come not . . . beshrew**
i.e., be careful you don't get put in Morel's skin, lest you curse yourself then
1084 **as** as if.   **wood** mad   1086 **I will . . . blood** i.e., I'll have your life
1087 **so have I bliss** as I hope to be saved   1091 **held with** sided with
1094 **lenger** longer   1098 **withouten miss** undoubtedly, certainly

Thus was Morel flain out of his skin   1103
To charm a shrew, so have I bliss.   1104
Forgive the young man if he did sin,
But I think he did nothing amiss.
He did all thing even for the best,
As was well provèd then.
God save our wives from Morel's nest!
I pray you say all Amen.

Thus ending the jest of Morel's skin,
Where the curst wife was lappèd in.
Because she was of a shrewd leer,   1113
Thus was she served in this manner.

He that can charm a shrewd wife
   Better than thus,
Let him come to me, and fetch ten pound
   And a golden purse.

This ballad, *A Merry Jest of a Shrewd and Curst Wife Lapped in Morel's Skin*, was printed by Hugh Jackson without date, c. 1550–1560. A single damaged copy is located in the Bodleian Library, Oxford. It has been reprinted by, among others, *The Shakespeare Society (London) Publications*, vol. 4, no. 25, London, 1844.

1103 flain flayed   **1104 charm** subdue.   **so have I bliss** as I hope to be saved   **1113 leer** disposition, countenance

Further Reading

Bean, John C. "Comic Structure and the Humanizing of Kate in *The Taming of the Shrew*." In *The Woman's Part: Feminist Criticism of Shakespeare*, ed. Carolyn Ruth Swift Lenz, Gayle Greene, and Carol Thomas Neely. Urbana, Chicago, and London: Univ. of Illinois Press, 1980. Bean admires the romantic element of the play—the process by which Kate comes to understand herself "through her discovery first of play and then of love"—but finds the taming offensive. He defends Kate's final speech as the expression of a nontyrannical hierarchy in which partners have distinctive but cooperative roles, but he argues that the process that brings Kate to speak it (like "a trained bear") is evidence of a "depersonalizing farce unassimilated from the play's fabliau source."

Berry, Ralph. "The Rules of the Game." *Shakespeare's Comedies: Explorations in Form*. Princeton, N.J.: Princeton Univ. Press, 1972. Throughout the play, Berry argues, different patterns of wooing parallel and contrast with each other. Petruchio and Kate's emerges as the healthiest of the play's relationships, for the "taming" is in reality the process by which a well-matched pair of lovers together work out an agreement "upon the rules of its games."

Charlton, H. B. *"The Taming of the Shrew." Shakespearian Comedy*, 1938. Rpt. London: Methuen; New York: Barnes and Noble, 1966. Charlton examines the structure of Shakespeare's comedy against the background of Renaissance Italian comic models (which are echoed in the Bianca–Lucentio subplot). In the Petruchio–Kate plot, however, Shakespeare moves beyond familiar romantic conventions, focusing instead upon the lovers' "matter-of-fact recognition of the practical and expedient."

Daniell, David. "The Good Marriage of Katherine and Petruchio." *Shakespeare Survey* 37 (1984): 23–31. Daniell discovers in the Kate–Petruchio plot surprising affinities with the language and experience of Shakespeare's early history plays. Daniell uses this insight to explore the play's theatricality—the "special ability of acting to embrace and give form to violence"—which provides the terms in which Kate and Petruchio find the means "of being richly together with all their contradictions—and energies—very much alive and kicking."

Evans, Bertrand. *Shakespeare's Comedies*, pp. 24–32. Oxford: Clarendon Press, 1960. Evans focuses on the contrast between the play's two plots: the minor plot depends upon the dynamics of "false supposes and unperceived realities," while Kate and Petruchio's full awareness of each other's nature, a trait that is unique among Shakespeare's comic lovers, forms the basis of the major plot.

Garber, Marjorie B. "Dream and Structure: *The Taming of the Shrew*." *Dream in Shakespeare: From Metaphor to Metamorphosis*. New Haven and London: Yale Univ. Press, 1974. For Garber, the induction introduces the play's thematic concern with appearance and reality. Sly's dream "distances later action and insures lightness of tone"; his transformation also prefigures and parallels Kate's, allowing us to see her change as a metamorphosis rather than a taming.

Hibbard, G. R. "*The Taming of the Shrew:* A Social Comedy." In *Shakespearean Essays*, ed. Norman Sanders and Alwin Thaler. Knoxville, Tenn.: Univ. of Tennessee Press, 1964. Hibbard's discussion of the marital customs of Elizabethan England suggests that the play is not only a dramatic exploration of romantic attitudes but also "an incisive piece of social criticism." Kate's frustrations emerge from actual social and economic conditions. Bianca and Lucentio reveal the shallowness of the conventional values of romance, while Kate's and Petruchio's "realistic" approach to life and love gives their marriage an appeal absent from the subplot.

Huston, J. Dennis. "Enter the Hero: The Power of the Play in *The Taming of the Shrew*." *Shakespeare's Comedies of Play*. New York: Columbia Univ. Press, 1981. Arguing that both the Induction and the marriage in mid-play subvert traditional comic conventions, Huston finds that Shakespeare's handling of literary tradition is analogous to Petruchio's treatment of Kate: Shakespeare animates sterile romantic conventions in the same way as Petruchio summons Kate out of her unthinking and automatic shrewishness "into the human theatre of play."

Kahn, Coppélia. "*The Taming of the Shrew*: Shakespeare's Mirror of Marriage." *Modern Language Studies* 5 (1975): 88–102. Rpt. in "Coming of Age: Marriage and Manhood in *Romeo and Juliet* and *The Taming of the Shrew*." *Man's Estate: Masculine Identity in Shakespeare*. Berkeley: Univ. of California Press, 1981. For Kahn, Kate's ironic submission liberates Petruchio from his stereotypic male dominance (reversing Huston's assessment; see above). The play satirizes not the shrewish female but the male desire to control women, and Kate's final speech not only "completes the fantasy of male domination but also mocks it as mere fantasy."

Leggatt, Alexander. "*The Taming of the Shrew*." *Shakespeare's Comedy of Love*. London: Methuen; New York: Barnes and Noble, 1974. Leggatt discovers the relationship between the induction and the play world in their common interest in "sport, playacting, and education." The Lord, Petruchio, and Kate herself have the "power to manipulate convention, to create experience rather than have experience forced upon them."

Nevo, Ruth. "Kate of Kate Hall." *Comic Transformations in Shakespeare*. London and New York: Methuen, 1980. Nevo admires the unconventional Petruchio as "stage manager and chief actor" of the play's psychodrama. His taming of Kate is an "instructive, liberating, and therapeutic" activity, which rescues her from an unenviable family situation in which her only defense is "her insufferability."

Saccio, Peter. "Shrewd and Kindly Farce." *Shakespeare Survey* 37 (1984): 33–40. Defending the farcical quality of the play, Saccio praises the energy, determination, and cleverness of the characters in remedying the static social world of Padua. Kate, he finds, is a participant rather than a victim of the farce, and her growing abilities as a farceur mark the stages of her liberation from a compulsive shrewishness.

Shaw, George Bernard. "*The Taming of the Shrew*." In *Shaw on Shakespeare*, ed. Edwin Wilson. New York: E. P. Dutton, 1961. Responding to a number of performances of the play, Shaw praises its "realistic" aspects. Petruchio rejects romantic affectation in favor of practical concerns for his own comfort. His taming of Kate is acceptable to an audience, since it is "good-humored and untainted by wanton cruelty." Nonetheless, Shaw is uncomfortable with Kate's final speech of submission: its "lord-of-creation moral," he asserts, is "disgusting to modern sensibility."

Tillyard, E. M. W. "The Fairy-Tale Element in *The Taming of the Shrew*." In *Shakespeare 1564–1964: A Collection of Modern Essays by Various Hands*, ed. Edward A. Bloom. Providence, R.I.: Brown Univ. Press, 1964. Tillyard presents several versions of shrew-taming folktales that may have served Shakespeare as sources, singling out the story of King Thrushbeard as the most likely analogue to the Kate plot and as a model for the induction.

Memorable Lines

I'll not budge an inch. (SLY   Ind.1.13)

Dost thou love pictures? We will fetch thee straight
Adonis painted by a running brook,
And Cytherea all in sedges hid,
Which seem to move and wanton with her breath.
(SERVANT   Ind.2.49–52)

Come, madam wife, sit by my side and let the world slip; we
shall ne'er be younger. (SLY   Ind.2.138–139)

No profit grows where is no pleasure ta'en.
In brief, sir, study what you most affect.
(TRANIO   1.1.39–40)

To seek their fortunes farther than at home,
Where small experience grows. (PETRUCHIO   1.2.50–51)

I come to wive it wealthily in Padua;
If wealthily, then happily in Padua. (PETRUCHIO   1.2.74–75)

Katharine the curst!
A title for a maid of all titles the worst.
(GRUMIO   1.2.128–129)

And do as adversaries do in law,
Strive mightily, but eat and drink as friends.
(TRANIO   1.2.276–277)

I am as peremptory as she proud-minded;
And where two raging fires meet together,
They do consume the thing that feeds their fury.
(PETRUCHIO   2.1.131–133)

BAPTISTA
    Why, then thou canst not break her to the lute?
HORTENSIO
    Why, no, for she hath broke the lute to me. (2.1.147–148)

KATHARINA
  They call me Katharine that do talk of me.
PETRUCHIO
  You lie, in faith, for you are called plain Kate.
                              (2.1.184–185)

And, will you, nill you, I will marry you.
                              (PETRUCHIO   2.1.268)

Kiss me, Kate, we will be married o' Sunday.
                              (PETRUCHIO   2.1.322)

Old fashions please me best.   (BIANCA   3.1.79)

. . . a little pot and soon hot.   (GRUMIO   4.1.5)

This is a way to kill a wife with kindness.
                              (PETRUCHIO   4.1.196)

He that knows better how to tame a shrew,
Now let him speak; 'tis charity to show.
                              (PETRUCHIO   4.1.198–199)

Our purses shall be proud, our garments poor,
For 'tis the mind that makes the body rich.
                              (PETRUCHIO   4.3.167–168)

Why, so this gallant will command the sun.
                              (HORTENSIO   4.3.192)

He that is giddy thinks the world turns round.
                              (WIDOW   5.2.20)

Fie, fie! Unknit that threatening unkind brow.
                              (KATHARINA   5.2.140)

A woman moved is like a fountain troubled,
Muddy, ill-seeming, thick, bereft of beauty.
                              (KATHARINA   5.2.146–147)

Contributors

DAVID BEVINGTON, Phyllis Fay Horton Professor of Humanities at the University of Chicago, is editor of *The Complete Works of Shakespeare* (Scott, Foresman, 1980) and of *Medieval Drama* (Houghton Mifflin, 1975). His latest critical study is *Action Is Eloquence: Shakespeare's Language of Gesture* (Harvard University Press, 1984).

DAVID SCOTT KASTAN, Professor of English and Comparative Literature at Columbia University, is the author of *Shakespeare and the Shapes of Time* (University Press of New England, 1982).

JAMES HAMMERSMITH, Associate Professor of English at Auburn University, has published essays on various facets of Renaissance drama, including literary criticism, textual criticism, and printing history.

ROBERT KEAN TURNER, Professor of English at the University of Wisconsin–Milwaukee, is a general editor of the New Variorum Shakespeare (Modern Language Association of America) and a contributing editor to *The Dramatic Works in the Beaumont and Fletcher Canon* (Cambridge University Press, 1966–).

JAMES SHAPIRO, who coedited the bibliographies with David Scott Kastan, is Assistant Professor of English at Columbia University.

❖

JOSEPH PAPP, one of the most important forces in theater today, is the founder and producer of the New York Shakespeare Festival, America's largest and most prolific theatrical institution. Since 1954 Mr. Papp has produced or directed all but one of Shakespeare's plays—in Central Park, in schools, off and on Broadway, and at the Festival's permanent home, The Public Theater. He has also produced such award-winning plays and musical works as *Hair, A Chorus Line, Plenty,* and *The Mystery of Edwin Drood,* among many others.

Shakespeare
ALIVE!

☐ 27081-8 $4.50/$5.50 in Canada

From Joseph Papp, America's foremost theater producer, and writer Elizabeth Kirkland: a captivating tour through the world of William Shakespeare.

Discover the London of Shakespeare's time, a fascinating place to be—full of mayhem and magic, exploration and exploitation, courtiers and foreigners. Stroll through narrow, winding streets crowded with merchants and minstrels, hoist a pint in a rowdy alehouse, and hurry across the river to the open-air Globe Theatre to the latest play written by a young man named Will Shakespeare.

SHAKESPEARE ALIVE! spirits you back to the very heart of that London—as everyday people might have experienced it. Find out how young people fell in love, how workers and artists made ends meet, what people found funny and what they feared most. Go on location with an Elizabethan theater company, learn how plays were produced, where Shakespeare's plots came from and how he transformed them. Hear the music of Shakespeare's language and the words we still use today that were first spoken in his time.

Open this book and elbow your way into the Globe with the groundlings. You'll be joining one of the most democratic audiences the theater has ever known—alewives, apprentices, shoemakers and nobles—in applauding the dazzling wordplay and swordplay brought to you by William Shakespeare.

Look for **SHAKESPEARE ALIVE!** at your local bookstore or use the coupon below:

the BANTAM *Shakespeare*

Bantam is proud to announce an important new edition of:

The Complete Works Of William Shakespeare

Featuring:

*The complete texts with modern spelling and punctuation

*Vivid, readable introductions by noted Shakespearean scholar David Bevington

*New forewords by Joseph Papp, renowned producer, director, and founder of the New York Shakespeare Festival

*Stunning, original cover art by Mark English, the most awarded illustrator in the history of the Society of Illustrators

*Photographs from some of the most celebrated performances by the New York Shakespeare Festival

*Complete source materials, notes, and annotated bibliographies based on the latest scholarships

*Stage histories for each play

ACCESSIBLE * AUTHORITATIVE * COMPLETE

SHAKESPEARE
The Complete works in 29 Volumes

Bantam Drama
Classics

☐	21279	Sophocles: Complete Plays	$3.25
☐	21219	Euripides: Ten Plays	$3.50
☐	21261	Aristophanes: Complete Plays	$3.95
☐	21280	Henrik Ibsen: Four Great Plays	$2.95
☐	21118	Rostand: Cyrano De Bergerac	$1.75
☐	21211	Anton Chekhov: Five Major Plays	$2.95

Buy them at your local bookstore or use this handy coupon for ordering:

BANTAM
SHOP~AT~HOME
C·A·T·A·L·O·G

Special Offer
Buy a Bantam Book
for only 50¢.

Now you can have Bantam's catalog filled with hundreds of titles plus take advantage of our unique and exciting bonus book offer. A special offer which gives you the opportunity to purchase a Bantam book for only 50¢. Here's how!

By ordering any five books at the regular price per order, you can also choose any other single book listed (up to a $5.95 value) for just 50¢. Some restrictions do apply, but for further details why not send for Bantam's catalog of titles today!

Just send us your name and address and we will send you a catalog!